SACRAMENTS
RITES OF PASSAGE

SACRAMENTS
RITES OF PASSAGE

by William J. O'Malley, S.J.

ThomasMore

A DIVISION OF TABOR PUBLISHING

Allen, Texas • Chicago, Illinois

Note: In quotations from certain sources, such words as "sons" or "mankind" or "men," which were commonplace at the time of their writing, have been changed to become more inclusive.

Send all inquiries to:
Thomas More Publishing
200 East Bethany Drive
Allen, Texas 75002–3804

Printed in the United States of America

ISBN 0–88347–293–7

1 2 3 4 5   99 98 97 96 95

To Kathleen and Richard Moon

TABLE OF CONTENTS

Chapter One

A WORLD
WITHOUT SINFUL
OR SACRED

Is that all there is?
Is that all there is?
If that's all there is, my friends,
    then keep on dancing.
    Let's break out the booze
    and have
    a ball.
        If that's all
        there is.

—*Peggy Lee*

A Puzzlement

One day an African pygmy boy was wandering in the forest when he suddenly stopped, spellbound by birdsong trilling in the trees somewhere overhead. The melody soared and swooped, warbled and cascaded, as if the soul of the bird herself were winging from her throat. And suddenly there she was, perched on a branch above his head, resplendent in feathers of blood red and iridescent blue. She cocked a quizzical eye at him and fluttered down to his bare shoulder, grasping it gently in her silver talons.

Gleefully the boy ran home with his prize, bursting into the hut just as his father returned, grim and empty-handed from the hunt. "Father," the boy cried, "look what I found! Isn't she beautiful? What shall we feed her?"

"Feed her?" his father growled. "What shall we feed your brothers and sisters? There is nothing!" And with that, the father grasped the bird from the boy's shoulder and strangled its cries. "Now," he said darkly, "we can live one more day."

But in killing the bird, he had killed the song. And in killing the song, he had killed himself.

Dehumanization

"Now what I want is Facts [Mr. Gradgrind told the teacher, Mr. McChoakumchild, and his quavering pupils]. Teach these boys and girls nothing but Facts. Facts alone are wanted in life. Plant nothing else, and root out everything else. You can only form the minds of reasoning animals upon Facts: nothing else will ever be of service to them. This is the principle on which I bring up my own children, and this is the principle on which I bring up these children. Stick to Facts, sir!"

–Charles Dickens, *Hard Times*

No room in Mr. Gradgrind's school for fancy, imagination, intuition, the unquantifiable, the "sense" of something larger than "Fact." In his school, a horse was not a noble beast, a snorting steed with flaring eyes, Bucephalus-Rocinante-Silver; it was "an equine quadruped." His students were not human spirits yearning for greatness, dreaming dreams, envisioning the unheard-of, exulting in the circus. They were "reasoning animals," to be sorted by his school into those capable of being managers and those destined to be no more than "the hands" in his mills. No sin in Mr. Gradgrind's school or world, except for sloth and lack of productivity. Nothing sacred except financial profit.

The progress of "civilization" has been, in a very real sense, a process of dehumanization. History is a story of disenchantments, not only in the sense of correcting naiveté, but of taking the magic out of everything.

In primitive cultures—some few of which still exist today in the outbacks of Australia and Brazil—the people's lives were surrounded and permeated by gods, magic, ritual, enchantment. They found their meaning and purpose, as tribes and as individuals, by interacting with the powerful forces of nature. The yearly *rhythm* of natural change gave a rhythm to their own lives—a sense of rightness, wholeness, meaning, like an artfully composed piece of music into which they blended. It gave a center to their lives, a connectedness, a shared vision, a *coherence*. For them, that relationship with nature and life was I-Thou and not I-It.

In later more civilized societies, Aztec and Maya, Egypt, Greece, and Rome, the forces of nature first became identified with anthropomorphic gods—Quetzalcoatl, Isis and Osiris, Hera and Zeus, Ceres and Vulcan. Then with the emergence of wealthy leisured classes, and thus an increase in sophisticated thought, the gods of Olympus began to seem almost embarrassing, a crude family of jealous manipulators—and the nature gods who preceded them seemed positively barbaric.

As philosophy and theology became more cerebral and rational, thinkers like Plato and Aristotle found earlier understandings of the divine in nature far too *immanent,* that is, too "locked within" this world. Rather they pictured the god as a distant creative intelligence in whom all the forces of the mind and the universe had their ideal and most real form.

Such a perfect god was too pure to become involved in the material world—nature—since that world was everywhere corruptible. Such a god was *transcendent,* infinitely removed from the everyday, and only in the most remote and imperfect way mirrored in immanent nature. It was this god of rarefied ideals who showed human beings, through reason, what was truly real, good, and beautiful: the meaning of human life.

And there you have the start of a most basic antagonism in ideas about the nature and purposes of the divinity—and thus the nature and purpose of humanity. Are nature—and human beings as part of that nature—everywhere alive with the immanent presence of divine power(s)? Or is corruptible matter/nature a prison in which some small sparks of transcendent divinity are trapped and seeking release? Or is it some unnerving combination of the two?

A bit earlier than Plato, in the Far East, a visionary named Guatama the Buddha had come to much the same conclusion, that the world of nature we *believe* is real is a delusion; the immanent is merely a trap for the transcendent, and the purpose of fulfilled human life is to deny the material and aspire to the nonphysical liberation of Nirvana, absorption into the Oversoul.

Meanwhile, along the eastern shore of the Mediterranean, there lived a people of quite different mind-set from their more sophisticated neighbors to the west and east: the Hebrews. They were far less heady than the Greeks in their ruminations about divinity and their divinely instituted purpose in life, and more down-to-earth than the Orientals. At the outset, they too had likely worshipped quite different primitive tribal gods, but then, overwhelmed by slavery in Egypt, they turned to a charismatic leader named Moses, who believed he had encountered the one and only God, Yahweh the Liberator, who dwelt with them and moved with them and protected them.

Their relationship with this God was far "warmer" than that of the Greeks to their distant First Cause or the Easterners to their impersonal Oversoul. For the Greeks, the truths of life were discerned through rigid logic and reasoning; for the Orientals in a total escape from that same calculating intelligence; for the Hebrews, truth was found not so much in the head as in the heart, not in logical exactitude nor in wordless contemplation, but in experience of trustworthiness.

For the Hebrews, the divine was incontestably holy and "other," yet they "knew" Yahweh also dwelt in the center of their city, in the Temple: transcendent, yet immanent. As they themselves became more sophisticated, rationalism also entered their understanding of God, not in the form of philosophy but rather in the exquisitely fine-tuning of the Law of their forefathers.

Then near the middle of what was to become the first century of a new era, news began to spread through the Mediterranean basin of a quite new and different understanding of God—and therefore of the meaning and purpose of human life. A new sect emerged from Judaism which claimed that the infinite God not only had created the world and given purpose to each of its parts, not only sent messages through privileged prophets, but this time the Divinity Itself had *entered* human history as a human being.

At the Incarnation, Divinity had somehow "emptied" itself of the use of divine power and become an individual human being, the transcendent totally immersed in the toil and sweat and frustration of immanent human life. *Emmanu-el,* God-with-us.

For centuries, philosophers argued as to how that could happen—a tripartite single God? Fully transcendent but completely immanent? And yet no matter how they argued, battled, connived against one another, all of them agreed that—somehow—the transcendent had fused with the immanent. Not just the divine power they sensed in the storm or the divine serenity they felt by a quiet lake, but God walking among us and living the kind of life God expected men and women to live. The sacred had become secular in order to make the secular sacred.

Then for thirteen centuries, from the conversion of Constantine to Christianity in 312 A.D. until the rise of Protestantism in the sixteenth century, the Catholic Church with its theology and ritual, saints and feast days, shrines and crusades, supplied the background matrix in which most of the European world found meaning and purpose. The *rhythm* of the liturgical year—from Christmas to Easter to Pentecost, with all kinds of saints' days in between—gave a background against which a community or an individual could judge whether they were "synchronized" with "the order of things."

The rhythm of the "peak moments" of their family lives—birth, puberty, marriage, moments of moral failure, death of loved ones—also found meaning in the sacraments of the Church, especially in the meal which celebrated their community and their inevitable triumph over suffering and death. Through the sacraments their needs and hopes passed upward to God and God's blessing passed downward to them. Even ravaged by plague, war, drought and invasion, life was ultimately "holy," ratified by the salvific blood of the Son of God, who had immersed himself in that same life. All the segmented joys and sufferings of their lives somehow "fit" into a coherent, meaningful pattern. To all intents and purposes, as for the pagan primitive, for thirteen centuries, the sacred and the secular were one life.

Then, for reasons too complex to ponder here, and with truth and wrongheadedness on each side, a major segment of the Christian Church cracked away from Roman Catholicism. A large part of the antagonism focused on that basic antagonism: the accessible immanent God vs. the inaccessible transcendent God, the divine we sense within the sacredness of nature vs. the divine which surpasses our comprehension. The Reformation, again, polarized Reality between a radically "other" and flawless Divinity on the one hand, and a radically corrupt humanity on the other.

The Reformation moved in reaction to real abuses that had turned the practices of the Church into mere superstition and magic—indulgences sold as ransom in the next life, relics as talismans against evil, and even the eucharist as somehow a "command" to God under an incantation to enter into the species of bread and wine. The Reformers reduced traditional religious expressions to the bare essentials, especially the sacraments. Only two remained: baptism and eucharist, both purged of most of the otherworldly elements centuries had invested them with. Baptism now effected no real inner change; the recipient remained as vile as a dunghill over which the merits of Christ were draped like concealing snow. The words of consecration effected no real inner change in bread and wine; they were merely symbols, reminders of Christ's passion and death and resurrection.

The disenchantment of the world and human life had begun.

Demythologizing

In his short story "The Grand Inquisitor," Fyodor Dostoevsky captures the extent to which, to many minds, the official Church had totally subverted the message of Jesus at the time of the Reformation. The old Inquisitor had captured Jesus on a day Jesus returned to Seville and immediately had him locked in prison before Jesus could ruin a system the old cardinal and others had carefully constructed to save pitiable human beings from the one gift which most terrified them: freedom, the need to think for themselves. In the temptations in the desert, the Enemy had offered Jesus the three means to capture the hearts and wills of men and women: miracle, mystery and power. Give them bread, dazzle them with magic, crush them with authority, and they will be happy, because they no longer need to think for themselves. Jesus had refused, but the Church—Dostoevsky says— set about to rectify the church by doing what Jesus would have done had he known better. Give them miracles in the sacraments; give them mystery in the richness of churches, incense, rich vestments; threaten them with power: the keys to heaven and hell.

Thus in the sixteenth and seventeenth centuries, a process of reform and disenchantment began outside the Church as well. The rise of empirical science began to show clear, this-world explanations for phenomena the preceding centuries had attributed to spirits and demons, to prayers answered or denied. Not magic, but cause and effect: reason. The Enlightenment—a movement of purely rationalist philosophers in Europe—set about to emancipate the world from the tyrannical dominance of priests and bishops and to demythologize the hocus-pocus with which they enslaved the illiterate, to substitute the rational for the "irrational." The so-called sacred was an obstacle to human freedom. Although the order of the universe convinced these men that there had to be an Ultimate Cause, an Architect, like Plato they believed this God far too perfect to concern himself with the mundane matters of daily life. There was no need to pray for divine intervention. That is why the Creator gave us intelligence, no matter how fearful we are of using it. There were now two totally separate worlds: the sacred and the secular.

In the New World, it was men of this mind, Deists, who successfully initiated the American Revolution, drew up a Constitution by which the new nation could define itself, and strictly separated the affairs of religion from the affairs of society. Many of them were also Freemasons and, as we shall see later, many of the American symbols we take for granted—like pictures even on a dollar bill—are the symbols of Freemasonry.

These disenchanting ideas spread all over Europe, chafing under the tyranny (not to mention the taxes) of the royal system on the one hand and the ecclesiastical system on the other. It culminated in the French Revolution in which kings and royal ministers, bishops and priests and nuns, were sent to the guillotine, and France was finally freed of structures of repression and the superstitions of peasantry. From then on, the so-called sacred would yield to the strictly secular. Pronouncements of emperors and kings were no longer validated by their delusive divinity; the individual conscience was no longer enslaved to the Grand Inquisitor; from now on, "Man is the measure of all things." One moment which captured that violent change was a woman, the Goddess of Reason, dancing naked on the high altar of the Cathedral of Notre Dame, before the shattered tabernacle. It was indeed a "New World" never before known.

Copernicus and Galileo had shown us we are not the center of the universe—nor even of this minor solar system. Later Darwin offered evidence that we, the fine flower of civilization, were quite likely only slightly improved apes. Then Freud showed that all the hopes and aspirations which keep us going are merely projections of the brute unconscious on a meaningless universe, and all the guilts that torment us and corrode what little life we have are not attributable to us but only to our inner blind unconscious and outer events in the world, neither of which we can control. There is no sin, only victimization.

> No, we have surmounted guilt. It's quite,
> Quite different, isn't it? You see the difference.
> Science knows now that the sentient spirit
> Floats like the chambered nautilus on a sea
> That drifts it under skies that drive:
> Beneath, the sea of the subconscious;
> Above, the winds that wind the world.
> Caught between that sky, that sea,
> Self has no will, cannot be guilty.
> —Archibald MacLeish, *J.B.*

Then, as the Industrial Revolution began to spread over the "civilized" world, when utilitarianism ("What works?") made far more rational sense than "irrational" altruism ("What's right?), Mr. Gradgrind came into his kingdom.

Fact is a verifiable quantity; "value" is nothing more than a man-made illusion. There will be no more "womanish" softness in what is the prime business of life: the interchange of goods and services and the accumulation of wealth. Today, in place of the hoodoo of primitive religions, in place of the childish gods of Greece and Rome, in place of Yahweh and the demystified Christ, in place even of the Goddess of Reason prancing on the altar of Notre Dame, we have a new god to give our lives meaning and purpose: the Economy.

The Myth of Secular Progress

In America, that hard-nosed, no-frills "religion" was first embodied in the Puritan, Cotton Mather: the way to righteousness is an upright character and hard work, "the Protestant work-ethic." Then it yielded to the practicality of Ben Franklin; to show how interchangeable Yankee shrewdness and "Christianity" have become in the American mind, many believe Franklin's dictum "God helps those who help themselves" actually comes from the Christian scriptures! That in turn devolved into the cynical advertising ploys of Phineas T. Barnum: "There's a sucker born every minute," and "You'll never go broke underestimating the American taste." And Barnum and Gradgrind are still riding high in the boardrooms of Madison Avenue, on the Tube, the billboards, the slide-out postcards in every magazine. Buy, buy, buy! You can't have too much.

Image is more important than substance; nothing succeeds like the appearance of success; it is not the gods that bestow success but consumption.

The Economy is its own justification. If it is good for the Economy, it is "of God."

The Law of the American Dream is more subtle in its statements and more sophisticated in its methods than the Law of the Jungle, but it is no less savage. It is less meticulous in its strictures than the Law of Moses, but it is no less demanding.

The following analogy of the Economy to idolatry might seem at first forced, but it will show how absolutely thoroughly the secular has replaced the sacred in every corner of our lives.

Just as the gods gave meaning and a sense of coherence and purposefulness to more primitive societies, and Yahweh made sense out of life for Hebrews, and Christ's message validated even suffering and death for the medieval and renaissance Church, now the Economy serves that purpose. A hundred years ago, the guidebook for "The Century of Progress Exhibition" stated: "Science discovers, genius invents, industry applies. And man adapts himself to, or is molded by, new things."

Our lives are validated only insofar as we become grist for the Gradgrind mill: workers, consumers, managers, investors—who serve the "priests": scientists, inventors, financiers, advertisers who answer our prayers for more "new things," which our ancestors could not have dreamed of, much less coveted.

And yet we are, most of us, willing devotees of the Idol, Economy. Many of us uncritically accept the values of the modern world: blind faith in technology, gadgets, progress, slavery to the electronic media. We are willing to accept that the "soul" of our society is not a shared spirit but a mass of electric circuits. Still, given the limits of the *Monopoly* game, we all benefit: the harder we work, the more we have to spend; the more we have to spend, the more the Economy thrives; the more the Economy thrives, the more we have to spend. And on it goes.

Ironically, this fanatic religious campaign has even been able, in a kind of *1984* "Newspeak," completely to turn around the very meaning of the word, "economy." Before, it had always meant thrift, conserving, buying carefully, frugality. Now it means precisely the opposite: expansion, spending, the bullish market, the golden calf. As with all religions, the economy through its advertisers is a work of *conversion,* a complete turnaround of values—even a complete inversion of what "value" now means.

Besides priests, there are highly valued "scriptures." For the hierarchy, there are *The Wall Street Journal* and *Forbes;* for the lower levels of the faithful, there are *People* and *Newsweek.* They tell us what's important and *who* is important, who are the "saints" who have "made it." And there are audiovisual "scriptures" as well, proclaiming the good news everywhere we turn: "THE MORE THINGS YOU HAVE, THE HAPPIER YOU'LL BE!" Like any religion, the Economy offers fulfillment: newer, improved, bigger, livelier lives. It has successfully evangelized and secularized not only institutions but the very *consciousness* of the "congregation"; we genuinely *want* what the "priests" and "scriptures" want us to want: more tangible proofs of our success. Thus, the supernatural and sacred are as nonsensical as astrology and fortune cookies.

No drill sergeant, no voodoo hypnotist, no Siberian brainwasher—not even Hitler or Big Brother—ever had such coverage, such compliant subjects, or such sophisticated and successful methods as the huckster-priests of the unquestioned Economy. And we don't mind, really, After all, it's good for all of us. It's very thorough evangelization.

The moral code of the idolatry is strict: work and compete, that is how you will find fulfillment, your real *value*—SAT's, report cards, salaries, promotions, new car, designer jeans (which used to be poor peoples' pants). Efficiency and speed become demigods in their own right, to the point that one would rather have a tried-and-true fast-food burger than enjoy a meal. On the assembly line, one plugs in this part to a piece someone else has assembled, hands it on to a faceless someone who paints it, who hands it on to someone else to ship, someone else to sell, someone else to drive. Soul-less, but efficient. But we all "profit."

As we will see later, there are also secular rituals that celebrate competition and the Economy: Super Bowls, Olympics, World Series in which sport is no longer sportive; Academy Awards, Emmys, Tonys, Grammys, Country Music Awards in which the point at issue is hardly art; political conventions in which the point is rarely character but more often image; rock concerts which are liturgies of the Id; shopping malls which are cathedrals of consumption. Even taking a walk is no longer a chance to "stop and smell the flowers" or sense the sacred in nature; that is short-circuited by the Walkman keeping us plugged in to "the divine."

One rarely-mentioned flaw in this secular religion (which amounts to a punishable heresy) is to observe that all the "saints" who have really devoted themselves wholeheartedly to the pursuit of its goals and promises, who have really "made it" in the idolatry of the Economy, so often find need to anaesthetize themselves from life with drugs and very frequently end up killing themselves: Elvis Presley, Marilyn Monroe, Janis Joplin, Jim Morrison, John Belushi, Howard Hughes, Jimi Hendrix, River Phoenix, Kurt Cobain, . . . and the beat goes on.

Despite the promises of the secular gospel, there was something missing from their lives which made them unable to accommodate "having it all," something integral and important. Perhaps what was lacking was a soul, a self. Perhaps they had "sold their souls"—their honest selves—to a false god.

With nothing but a calculatedly "soulless" background against which to measure themselves—unlike the sacred myth systems of the primitive, the ancient, the Hebrew, the Catholic—the modern man or woman finds life segmented, one-damn-thing-after-the-other, with no sense of meaningful coherence, no storyline. The surgeon often treats us merely as biological specimens in need of repair, the politician as so many votes to open a door and then be forgotten, a general as so many dogfaces to accomplish a task rather than sons and daughters and wives and husbands of somebody. The battle-weary teacher can deal with so many (admittedly peevish) human beings as so many educands to get through the system, and the Economy's Gradgrinds can treat human beings as if they were merely "economic factors."

For all our speed and efficiency, for all our goods and services, for all our defenses against even inconvenience, for all our better nutrition and medical care and life-expectancy, are we demonstrably any *happier* than the primitive squatting among so many enchantments, the Hebrew clutching his prayer shawl and muttering prayers to Yahweh, the medieval peasant leaning her hoe on the furrow to say the Angelus? Do we have a more genuine sense of self, a more heartfelt sense of belonging to a community and a cause greater than the limits of our own skins, a true sense of living purposeful lives—than those simpler folk, benighted in simplicity, superstition, and magic? Are we missing something?

The world to which unbalanced rationalism has led us, the demystified world given us by the Enlightenment and Scientism, the utilitarian world of Gradgrind and Barnum and the Economy seems a cold place indeed. It is empirical, this-worldly, secular, pragmatic, contractual, hedonistic, disenchanted. "Is that all there is?" Something seems to be missing, something integral and important.

> We are the hollow men
> We are the stuffed men
> Leaning together
> Headpiece filled with straw.
> Alas!
> —T. S. Eliot, *The Hollow Men*

The curse of liberated modern society seems to be a sense of short-term goals and long-term aimlessness. Yet the quest for Eden, for "home," is the root of human history—the pioneers, our grandparents who set sail for the New World, our parents who fought World Wars to build security not for themselves but for their children. They had an intuitive "sense" things could be better: a dream to validate their lives, and in the going, they were "already there."

But, since the 60s, we have been derailed from questing into a kind of dull resignation, from striving to mere survival. Our hearts are not restless; just frustrated, by our inescapable but unfed hunger. Yet it is precisely our stubborn refusal to adapt, our snotty conviction we could prevail, which *made* us human and keeps us human. When we let it go, our humanity—and the humanity of our cities—slips away with it. No need for more evidence of that dull resignation to a life without hope than the surly attendant who shoves change at you in the subway.

Now, only one goal: more. Once our hero was a farmboy named Lincoln, for whom the human appetite had a goal: human dignity. Now our hero is a farmboy named Presley, who "had it all" but killed himself. Yet years later, 2,000 people visit his shrine every day.

If the agents of the Economy have the answers, why are millions in third-generation Welfare? Why do so many wander streets, with dead-end eyes, bumming change and sleeping on grates? Why so many divorces, so many suicides, especially among teenagers who "have it all"? Why do the young, who used to embody our hope, drop out, turn to drugs and crime? Why do the privileged cling to cool, indifference, disconnectedness? Why do we all settle for bland food, education, TV, liturgy? Why do half our citizens find voting not worth the effort?

Something seems to be missing. Something integral and important.

Cosmos and Chaos

As Gregor Samsa awoke one morning from uneasy dreams, he found himself transformed in his bed into a gigantic insect. He was lying on his hard, as it were armor-plated, back and when he lifted his head a little he could see his domelike brown belly divided into stiff arched segments on top of which the bed quilt could hardly keep in position and was about to slide off completely. His numerous legs, which were pitifully thin compared to the rest of his bulk, waved helplessly before his eyes.

—Franz Kafka, *The Metamorphosis*

Even though he has just awakened to find he is now an enormous cockroach, Gregor, a traveling salesman, lies helplessly on his back, trying occasionally to turn over, ruminating: "And apart from the business itself, this plague of traveling, the anxieties of trains, the irregular, inferior meals, the ever-changing faces, never to be seen again, people with whom there was no chance to be friendly. To *hell* with it!"

He thinks he might just go to the boss and quit. But his parents owe the boss money, and he's the sole support of his family. His father is retired and fat, his mother asthmatic, his sister, Greta, too young and delicate. Here he has just become a huge piece of vermin, and all he can think of is how vexed his boss will be that he missed his train! Yet what's the difference? He's been as insignificant as a cockroach all his life.

His parents and his sister knock on the locked door, and he tries to answer. What he says is intelligible to him, but all they hear is squeals. His boss shows up and hammers on the door. "Did you understand a word?" he asks Gregor's parents. "It was an animal's voice." But even the day before, Gregor had been of little more importance to the boss than a function, a cockroach.

Finally, Gregor manages to turn the key with his jaws, and the door opens. The people outside are thunderstruck. They hound him back into his room and lock the door from outside.

Gregor realizes that "his duty was to remain docile and try to make things bearable for his family." His sister dutifully leaves a bowl of milk and bread inside the door, but it revolts him. All he can eat is garbage. No one suspects he can understand them, so no one tries to communicate to him. So he creeps to the door in the evening to listen to his family's conversation at dinner or pushes the chair to the window to stare out, every day more shortsighted until the world is "all grey desert." He lies there all day, surrounded by filth and his own droppings.

But his weakness seems to invigorate the family: his father becomes a bank guard, his mother takes in sewing, his sister accepts a position in a shop. To make ends meet, they admit three gentlemen boarders who take over the apartment while the family is forced to live in the kitchen.

One evening after supper, his sister plays the violin for the boarders, and drawn by the beauty of the music, Gregor moves toward the door that has mistakenly been left ajar. And he edges on his many legs out into the room. The three gentlemen boarders see him, horrified, and flee to their rooms, refusing to pay the rent and threatening a lawsuit.

His sister, who had been so solicitous for him, finally wails that she can't go on. "We've got to get rid of it! It's *not* Gregor!" Crushed, he crawls grimly back to his room and lies there, panting, and finally his head falls forward and he breathes his last. When his family are finally rid of him, they decide to take a day's trip into the countryside. And all they can think of is that it's time to find a husband for Greta.

Gregor has committed the unforgivable sin: trying to replace his father as head of the house, trying to be a self in an anthill. As a result, he is "put in his place"; something monstrous—but nonetheless real—has happened to him. He's become an insect, an automaton, a slave of instincts and of other people. His attitude to dirt changes; he begins to take pleasure in crawling; he becomes degraded and infantile. Which is what he has been all along: a modern man, alienated and estranged.

He is totally dehumanized, and all he can think of is the weather, his job, a missed train and—most pressingly—how to turn over and get out of bed. Yet what has happened to him is unthinkable, intolerable, therefore it can't be true. All will be well, and then he will simply take a later train. Gregor has found himself in a nightmare world in which nothing horrible is impossible. His cosmos has collapsed into chaos.

From time immemorial, as we saw, widely separated all over the globe, early societies tried to make sense of the world—find a perspective against which they could measure their everyday lives—by a combination of stories woven into their society's myth. Archaeologists, social historians, students of comparative religions, and psychologists find an astonishing consistency in elements which recur from one myth system to another—even though the peoples were separated by continents and oceans and thousands of years: Babylonian, Aztec, Laplander, Egyptian, Polynesian, Native American, African, Eskimo.

Although the specific images may differ, all seem to agree that in the beginning there was chaos; it might have been the roiling of sky waters and earth waters, a horrific monster, or as in the Hebrew scriptures, a dark Void (*chaos,* gas). But some god or gods struggled against the chaos or monster and out of it created cosmos: the ordered dance of the universe they saw year after year, the cycle of seasons, the predictable passages in life from birth through weaning and schooling to adolescence and on into adulthood, old age, and death. (What is unique about the Judeo-Christian-Islamic God is that there is no struggle; God brings cosmos out of chaos merely by willing it.)

What has happened now that the purely rationalist Myth of Economic Progress has demythologized and disenchanted us (in both senses of the word) from the sacred elements of those ancient myths? We are left with . . . nothing. If nothing I do is sacred or sinful, then nothing I do has any importance at all. I am, despite my hope, as negligible as Gregor Samsa. "Is that all there is? Then keep on dancing, let's break out the booze and have a ball, if that's all . . . there is."

Although—even in the modern secularized society—few would admit to atheism, an alarming number of people, young and old, at least seem to *act* as if "that's all there is": five days of meaningless work, meaningless study, meaningless competition, and two days to "break out the booze and have a ball."

> Ah, love, let us be true
> To one another! for the world, which seems
> To lie before us like a land of dreams,
> So various, so beautiful, so new,
> Hath really neither joy, nor love, nor light,
> Nor certitude, nor peace, nor help for pain;
> And we are here as on a darkling plain
> Swept with confused alarms of struggle and
>   flight,
> Where ignorant armies clash by night.
>   —Matthew Arnold, *Dover Beach*

Shakespeare's *Macbeth,* no mean world-beater himself, put the same truth less wistfully and more grimly:

> Tomorrow, and tomorrow, and tomorrow,
> Creeps in this petty pace from day to day
> To the last syllable of recorded time,
> And all our yesterdays have lighted fools
> The way to dusty death. Out, out, brief
>   candle!
> Life's but a walking shadow, a poor player
> That struts and frets his hour upon the
>   stage

And then is heard no more; it is a tale
Told by an idiot, full of sound and fury,
Signifying nothing.

Here we stand, hapless, hopeless, hairless apes stranded in a remote corner of a mindless reality.

Atheism

One of the best ways actually to experience and feel the truth of a world without sinful or sacred, a reality in which we can—or have to—get along without God is in Samuel Beckett's absurdist tragicomedy *Waiting for Godot*. Each night, two bums named Didi and Gogo meet at a nearly leafless tree in an empty place to wait for Godot—God, or death, or some kind of answer that will make sense of their meaningless routine lives. They are two halves of a nonentity, filling the time with absurdities, verbal ping-pong, anything—as the Grand Inquisitor says—to keep from thinking. They fuss with their hats and shoes, discuss suicide, ramble on about their day—which was the same as the last and the one before, They encounter Pozzo and Lucky, who are on the move and making progress—in a circle.

GOGO: Let's go.
DIDI: We can't.
GOGO: Why not?
DIDI: We're waiting for Godot.
GOGO: (despairingly) Ah! (Pause.) You're sure it was here.
DIDI: What?
GOGO: He said by the tree. (They look at the tree.) Do you
　　　see any others? . . .

DIDI: What are you insinuating? That we've come to the wrong place?

GOGO: He should be here.

DIDI: He didn't say for sure he'd come.

GOGO: And if he doesn't come?

DIDI: We'll come back to-morrow.

GOGO: And then the day after to-morrow.

DIDI: Possible.

GOGO: And so on.

DIDI: The point is—

GOGO: Until he comes.

GOGO: You're merciless.

DIDI: We came here yesterday . . .

Round and round, killing time while waiting for time to kill them. "Blathering about nothing in particular." Waiting. Hoping. Against all hope. Act after act. Night after night. Year after year.

DIDI: Was I sleeping while the others suffered? Am I sleeping now? To-morrow, when I wake, or think I do, what shall I say of to-day? That with Estragon my friend, at this place, until the fall of night, I waited for Godot? That Pozzo passed, with his carrier, and that he spoke to us? Probably. But in all that what truth will there be? (Gogo, having struggled with his boots in vain, is dozing off again. Didi looks at him.) He'll know nothing. He'll tell me about the blows he received and I'll give him a carrot. (Pause.) Astride of a grave and a difficult birth. Down in the hole, lingeringly, the grave-digger puts on the forceps. we have time to grow old. The air is full of our cries. (He listens.) But habit is the great deadener. (He looks again at Gogo.) At me too someone is looking, of me too someone is saying, He is sleeping, he knows nothing, let him sleep on. (Pause.) I can't go on! (Pause.) What have I said?

And so it goes. Act after act. Night after night. Year after year. Finally, at the end of the second act (as almost identically as the end of the first act):

GOGO: Why don't we hang ourselves?
DIDI: With what?
GOGO: You haven't got a bit of rope?
DIDI: No.
GOGO: Then we can't.
    (Silence.)
DIDI: Let's go.
GOGO: Wait, there's my belt.
DIDI: It's too short.
GOGO: You could hang on my legs.
DIDI: And who'd hang on mine.
GOGO: True.
DIDI: Show all the same. (Gogo loosens the cord that holds up his trousers which, much too big for him, fall about his ankles. They look at the cord.) It might do in a pinch. But is it strong enough?
GOGO: We'll soon see. Here. (They each take an end of the cord and pull. It breaks. They almost fall.)
DIDI: Not worth a curse.
    (Silence.)
GOGO: You say we have to come back to-morrow?
DIDI: Yes.

GOGO: Then we can bring a good bit of rope.

DIDI: Yes.

   (Silence.)

GOGO: Didi.

DIDI: Yes.

GOGO: I can't go on like this.

DIDI: That's what you think.

GOGO: If we parted? That might be better for us.

DIDI: We'll hang ourselves tomorrow. (Pause.) Unless
   Godot comes.

GOGO: And if he comes?

DIDI: We'll be saved.

GOGO: Well? Shall we go?

DIDI: Pull on your trousers.

GOGO: What?

DIDI: Pull on your trousers.

GOGO: You want me to pull off my trousers?

DIDI: Pull ON your trousers.

GOGO: (realizing his trousers are down) True. (He pulls up
   his trousers.)

DIDI: Well? Shall we go?

GOGO: Yes, let's go.

   (They do not move.)

   (Curtain)

Beckett captures, with whimsical gloom, life without God,
without sinful or sacred, but also stripped of all the noise and
busyness and short-range goals with which we populate our lives
("Habit is the great deadener") and keep ourselves from thinking
much beyond the present moment. Surely not thinking to the
end of our lives—whenever that unpredictable event will be.

What happens then? Do we go on, or "Is that all there is?" It's one or the other. And no matter how we distract ourselves from that question, no matter how we'd prefer not to consider it at all, it is the most *crucial* question of all: the question of my own ultimate personal value. *Either* I will go on, which means that there must be "some" transcendent reality beyond this life, *or* I will not go on, and I am just so much garbage waiting for the pick-up day. "Astride of a grave and a difficult birth. Down in the hole, lingeringly, the grave-digger puts on the forceps."

Oh, the God question is important all right. Because the God question is the Me question. "God is dead; we live in the post-Christian era." The death of God is really the death of humanity, because without a God—or *something* bigger than this life which leads inevitably to death—I am ultimately nothing. There is no meaning to terms like "value" or "love" or "soul" outside their temporary material meanings. Life is a kaleidoscope of disjointed experiences, various beads without a string. Any experience is as meaningful as any other. Or meaningless.

As Albert Camus said, in a godless universe the two greatest curses are intelligence and hope. Evolution took one blind, cruel step too far and came up with a species which yearns for answers and yearns to survive death. But without God there are no ultimate answers, and no one gets out alive. We are the only species we know cursed with a hunger for food that does not exist. By the sheer accident of birth—for which none of us was in any way responsible—we are condemned to death and extinction. Mother Teresa and Times Square pimps will receive the same "reward": annihilation. As Pozzo says, "That's how it is on this bitch of an earth."

Meanwhile, without a larger background against which to judge my ultimate value, I am—like Didi and Gogo—merely an improvisational self, out here on an empty stage, waiting for someone to come on and give me reason for dialogue, yearning for a Director. And there is none. "At me too someone is looking." Surely there *must* be! No. Not if that's all there is.

It is a very grim realization, but if there is no God, no transcendent dimension to human life, there is *no* other alternative. Facing that inevitable truth, Didi says, "I can't go on!" And then almost immediately, "What have I said?" And Gogo later says, "I can't go on like this." And Didi says, "That's what you think."

With their pants-dropping clownishness, they are ridiculous. And there's not even Anyone to laugh at them. As Woody Allen said, "Not only is God dead, but try to get a plumber on the weekend."

Given the only other alternative, God and the transcendent and the sacred seem perhaps worth another consideration.

Reductionism

In order to understand things better, we set them off against their opposites and contrast them as if they really were completely independent of one another.

> masculine/feminine
> left brain/right brain
> black/white
> good/evil
> flesh/spirit
> reason/intuition
> animate/inanimate
> this-world/other-world
> mortal/immortal
> sacred/secular

But in concrete reality they're not as easily separable. Male/female, for instance, is an objective fact and instantly clear; just lift the diaper and there you have it. "Masculine/feminine," not so. If by "masculine" (as opposed to "male") we mean those qualities associated with the left brain—logic, calculation, decisiveness, etc., then Margaret Thatcher is far more "masculine" than June Cleaver, yet they are both females. If by "feminine" we mean those qualities associated with the right brain—intuition, inclusiveness, the ability to see a problem in context rather than in left brain isolation, Alan Alda is far more "feminine" than Norman Mailer, though both are male.

In reality, objects are rarely indilutedly black or white; good can beget evil and evil can result in good. An ill-adjusted spirit can inflict psychosomatic diseases on the body, and many physicians agree, a vibrant psyche can also have a strong effect on healing the body. It may be a handy way to discuss the operations of the human mind by restricting reason to the left lobe which calculates and measures, and intuition to the right lobe that has hunches and envisions the not-yet-real, but Michelangelo—for all his intuitive genius—was also a superb draftsman: a single and unfragmented human being. To our quite limited eyes, a rock *appears* to be just that: inanimate, unmoving, inert, and yet it is actually aswarm with galaxies of whizzing particles. More "alive" than we realize. If there indeed is a God and if we will indeed survive death, then even people in mortal danger of death are actually immortal, right now, even as they die. If Christianity is true, then the sacred and secular are no longer as easily separable; the transcendent God became not only immanent but visible and tangible.

Reality—immanent or transcendent—is far, far more complex than our simple mutually exclusive divisions, more complex even than our most erudite science or philosophy or theology. Since 1932 when Werner Heisenberg won the Nobel Prize for Physics for enunciating the Principle of Uncertainty, we know the atom looks nothing at all like the handy Nils Bohr model of pellets whirling about a solid nucleus; sometimes an electron acts like a pellet, sometimes like a wave. At the end of his life, Thomas Aquinas himself said that—compared to the Reality—his lifetime of philosophizing and theologizing about God was "straw."

In order to understand, we have to simplify. The problems arise when we oversimplify.

"Reductionism" describes attempts to understand reality— whether in science, philosophy, or theology—which *over*simplify, which leave out pertinent data. Mr. Gradgrind, for instance, described the pupils in his school as "reasoning animals," which is the same term philosophy has used from Plato through medieval and renaissance theologians to the utilitarians of the eighteenth century: *animal rationale.* But that reductionist defi- nition—and all the theories spun out from it—limits human beings to nothing more than apes with implanted computers, bodies with nothing more than the calculating, rationalist, logical powers of the left brain. That leaves out one whole lobe of the brain, the one associated with dreaming, having hunches, creating art and music, falling in love—none of which is any way logical or "rational." They are not *ir*rational, but they are *non*- rational. What even theologians left out of the definition of humanity was the one thing which separates us from animals and which survives material death: the soul—conscience-self-spirit— who-we-are.

As far as we know, no lioness attacks a gazelle and then lumbers back to the jungle moaning, "Oh, *God!* I did it *again!*

I've got to get counselling!" Good human beings do; bad human beings don't. That's how you tell good human beings from bad human beings: good human beings feel remorse; bad human beings act no better than animals who never activated their uniquely human potential. The lioness is just following her nature; the bad human being is refusing to follow his or hers.

Literalism is also a form of reductionism, whether it is used cynically, as in Scientism, or used credulously, as in Fundamentalism. Literalism removes all the overtones, connotations, suggestiveness of words and limits them to their strict, left-brain-only dictionary definitions. Scientism looks at the scripture and, taking Elijah's fiery chariot and Jesus' walking on the water literally, dismisses them (and the rest of scripture) as so much naive primitive raving. Fundamentalism looks at scripture and, taking the serpent in Eden and angels at Bethlehem literally, is forced to deny (or put into a sealed room of the brain) everything we know from evolution, physics, psychology, and zoology: somehow there was a time when a snake *did* actually talk and the sky over Bethlehem actually *was* filled with fiery physical beings who had flown across the cold of space and were singing away without anyone in the town hearing them but a group of shepherds in the fields.

Symbolism, however, as we will see far more extensively later, opens up the events and statements of the scriptures to more than mere strict and sole left brain understanding. The authors of Genesis and their audience, for instance, did not believe animals once talked to humans, any more than Aesop who was writing about the same time. The snake was not *literal* but a multi-faceted *symbol* for temptation: an agent both loathsome and fascinating, ready to attack the unwary, but also the ritual symbol of the Canaanite fertility cults which surrounded

Hebrews for centuries and were constantly luring away the susceptible.

The rationalism we have seen grow and ultimately triumph in Western society—and now in the Far East, Near East, and Africa, and South America because of electronic communication—is also an example of reductionism. The factor which all the rationalist dogmas and theories and decisions leave out of the equation entirely is a most important factor: humanity.

Something within me rebels—as fiercely as I would rebel against being forced into slavery—against a system or a society or a myth which regards me and treats me as no more than an ape with a computer implanted.

[Read the following aloud and see if it holds true for you as well.] I am *not* just a biological specimen or a vote-caster or a dogface or an educand or an "economic factor." I am *not* just a tangle of horny loins connected by a reptilian brain stem to the brain of a rapacious wolf. I am *not* just so much potential garbage waiting to be picked up, *not* just a sack of chemicals or a higher-level beast, *not* just a snarl of blind inner drives. Jesse Jackson says it: "I . . . am . . . *somebody!*"

There is something within me that can't be reduced to flesh and brain, chemicals and electricity. There is something very real in me that dreams, hopes, falls in love—against all rationality—and with *this* person, yearns for respect, demands justice, longs to feel a sense of rhythm in my life that gives it meaning and coherence and purpose. That something very real *totally* eludes the concern and categories of rationalism, goes completely beyond the "empirical, this-worldly, secular, pragmatic, contractual, hedonistic, disenchanted."

That something is my soul. And if I have to submit to the possibility that, because it raises me above the level of a mere ape,

I am capable of a sinfulness no ape could comprehend—then so be it. And if I have to submit to a God whose purposes I can't always comprehend in order to have a sense that, in the end, everything I suffer does have a purpose—then so be it.

I yield to the sinful and the sacred because the *reductio ad absurdum* of rationalist reductionism, the world without either guilt or a sense of the holiness of humanity, is Auschwitz.

The *Reductio ad Absurdum*

During World War II, the Nazis gassed and worked to death not only six million Jews but at least ten million Slavs as well. Gas accounted for "relatively few" deaths; by far the majority were overworked and starved to death. The Nazis eliminated at least 150,000 homosexuals and about as many Gypsies, as "Untermenschen," less than human. There were at least 2,700 priests in the Dachau concentration camp alone, half of whom died.

But these men and women could not be allowed to sit around idle; they were valuable commodities in a rational economy. Thus they were rented out as slaves to German war industries in the area: BMW, Messerschmidt, Krupp, I. G. Farben—many of them still quite profitable businesses today and contributing their fair share to the German Economy and to the nation in taxes.

Manpower meant money. A prisoner bookkeeper in the Labor Office of the Dachau Camp found and kept a record showing just how valuable each of these worthless men and women was to the Third Reich.

(RM = Reichsmarks.)

Daily rental of prisoner	+ RM	6.00
Deduction for food	– RM	.60
Deduction for use of clothes	– RM	.10
Value of prisoner per days	+ RM	5.30
x Usual lifespan (270 days) =	+ RM	1,431.00
Average proceeds from rational disposal of corpse (fillings, clothes, bones, valuables held by bursar)	+ RM	200.00
	+ RM	1,631.00
Cost of cremation	– RM	2.00
Total value of prisoner	+ RM	1,629.00

Note that the usual lifespan was 270 days: nine months. But some lived longer, as long as four or five years, worth nearly 10,000 Reichsmarks. Note also that this economy was most economical, even extracting their now useless teeth-fillings, using their hair for mattress stuffing, and their bones for fertilizer.

That, to the rational economics of the Third Reich was the "value" of a human being, each of whom was a son or daughter of someone, each of whom had dreams and hopes and a need for respect. Each of whom had a soul, a self. But not in the Third Reich. *Untermenschen*. Gregor Samsas. Rational animals.

"Is that all there is?"

Chapter Two

ANIMATING THE HUMAN SOUL

I am a part of all that I have met;
Yet all experience is an arch wherethrough
Gleams that untraveled world, whose
      margin fades
For ever and for ever when I move.
How dull it is to pause, to make an end,
To rust unburnished, not to shine in use!
As though to breathe were life!
                —*Alfred, Lord Tennyson, Ulysses*

A Puzzlement

*Am I the bulb that carries the light, or am I the
light of which the bulb is the vehicle?*

—Joseph Campbell

Conversion to Humanity

As we have seen, we are free to treat one another—and ourselves—
as if we were nothing more than mere animals with computers
implanted in their heads. But that is self-evidently *not* all that we
are. We know we are not angels, but we also know we are not
sharks or spinach or stepping stones. There is something in each
of us which is *more* than the physical hungers of the body for
food, exercise, sex, sleep, and *more* than the mental hungers of
the mind for facts, gossip, definitions, causes and effects, distractions. There are hungers that simply can't be reduced to the
physical or mental: unselfish love, honor, imagination, music,
dreams, awe, trust, freedom, dignity—none of which is "rational,"
none of which was taught in Mr. Gradgrind's school—or in most
schools. Nor is our concern yet with the soul and religion, just
with the soul and *humanity.* Until the human soul begins to
evolve, religion has no chance.

What separates us from even the most intelligent animals is
not the body or brain (which they share). What separates us—by
a quantum leap—is the soul. No matter where it's "located," it is
undeniably there, and we have seen extensively what happens
when an individual or society *denies* it is there.

But what *is* the soul?

It may come as a bit of a shock, but no one sees you! Not that you're invisible, but the only thing they can see is your body. They don't see who-you-are; they don't see your *self*. They can look at the way you use your body, what you wear, assess what you talk about, and make educated guesses about the "you" inside. But that's all they are, guesses. Even we ourselves would be hard-pressed to "capture" in words who we really are. The reason is, first, that the soul—the "me"—is elusive, incapable of showing up on an x-ray plate. But more important, finding one's soul requires effort, and most of us have more important things to do than find out who we are, where we've been, where we're going. We just . . . go on. Which is a good reason to write an autobiography, no matter how painstaking the task, because without a sense of "self," our days are nothing more than odd beads without a string to tie them together.

You know someone is alive when their breath fogs a mirror. That breath is a sure sign at least the body is alive. In Hebrew, Greek, and Latin, the word for "breath" is the same as the word for "spirit, soul": *ruah, pneuma, anima.* Soul is the "aliveness" in each of us. When someone dies, something that was there before is gone; the body is there, but the *person* is not. Either the person is "somewhere else" or the person no longer *is*. Even hundreds of thousands of years ago, neanderthals buried their dead with weapons and provisions, because they believed the soul—the person—was on a journey into another way of existing.

The soul is the whole scheme of *values* that gives a sense of rootedness to life. It feeds on the outer world and digests what it finds to form wisdom and character. "Personality" is on the outside; a defense; "character" is on the inside: the true self—if, in fact, there is one. The soul holds together body and mind into a coherent whole. But the soul—the self—is not a destination to be attained and conquered once for all; it is a *process* of becoming, a journey. The soul is not a map; it is a compass. Activating one's soul is a decision, a *conversion,* a new way of seeing—not just the rational left brain counting the costs, figuring the odds, guarding the self, but the intuitive right brain "sensing" the "rightness" of one's choices, one's direction, one's whole life.

Sigmund Freud enunciated what he called "The Pleasure Principle." Each of us, he claimed, is in tension between two inner forces: *Eros,* the life wish, and *Thanatos,* the death wish. Eros, the life wish, craves challenge, commitment at risk, the journey—as with Tennyson's Ulysses. Thanatos, the death wish, craves security, being unbothered, a return to the womb. The healthy psyche (soul, self) can be drawn by the life wish, in even the smallest challenges of living, to hazard the good we have in the hope of something better. Granted that the urge to go *beyond* can be perverted into a life of gambling or death-defying stunts. But that is the life wish warped into validating the self from *outside:* how I can put other people down, how I can get people to accept me for broken records, how I can impress people by my external "lifestyle." The true life wish is the urge to become a better *self,* to be fully conscious of oneself as a *human* being.

Nietszche said anyone with a *why* to live for could endure just about any *how,* and Viktor Frankl's book, *Man's Search for Meaning,* shows that, even in Nazi prison camps, under the most antihuman conditions, women and men kept hold of their souls because they had a *reason* to: a loved one, a religious faith, a commitment to a cause—anything larger than the limits of their skins. Others "sold their souls," licked boots in order to survive, and died inside themselves—even though their bodies continued to move. A soul can be surrendered, but it can never be *taken* away. But without that inner compass, life is "a tale told by an idiot, full of sound and fury, signifying nothing."

The Potential Soul

In the first chapter, we saw the results of the soul-less society which treats men and women as if they, too, were soul-less. We saw what happens to individuals who merely "react" to life, letting it "happen to" them: Elvis and Marilyn, Gregor and his family, Didi and Gogo, the assembly line automaton and the grim subway changemaker. One is tempted to believe such people did not "lose" their souls or "sell" them. Rather they never really *had* their souls in the first place. They each had a surface "personality"—and often a very marketable one, but they lacked the inner "character" to deal with life with both feet planted on the ground, refusing to be treated—or treat themselves—with less dignity than a human being deserves.

It is easy to see the difference between "personality" and "character." "She has a lot of personality" means she has the ability to charm, beguile, engage attention. "She has a lot of character" is something quite different; she has a kind of rooted-ness, self-confidence, the ability to weather whatever comes. Personality is external; character is within.

Personality is a set of habits we unconsciously and reactively develop (usually before age three) in order to cope with the particular set of parents and siblings we accidentally happened to have been born into: aggressive or defensive, introverted or extroverted; shy, confident, vain, humble, sensitive, coarse, etc., in response to the family's being warm or chill, demanding or yielding, caring or indifferent, etc.

No particular personality type is "better" than any other; each has its assets and liabilities. Nor is anyone "responsible" for his or her personality type—at least in the sense that he or she "chose" it. The habits of one's personality *were* formed, in a small child, without any reasoned choice. But when one comes into adolescence, able to reason and ponder, capable of taking charge of his or her own life, then he or she does become responsible for what they *do with* the personality they have. That is the time when each of us is "invited" to form a personally validated self—a character, a soul, a self.

But it is an invitation which—as we have seen—many refuse. Many—perhaps most—potential human beings can content themselves with getting by on personality, image, making a living and then dying, without ever finding out what living was for.

Baby : Cub = Acorn : Marble

A human infant and a bear cub look, at first, quite similar; so do an acorn and a marble. But there is a really a quantum difference between each of the pairs. You can bury the acorn and the marble, and the marble is just going to lie there. It hasn't the *potential* to be anything more than what it is. But the acorn has the potential to become hugely different from what it is: an oak reaching fifty feet in the air and nearly as far underground. That need not happen. It can fall into water and rot, lie rootless on rock, take root and then wither in drought. Its potential needn't be activated.

The same is true of the human infant and the bear cub. At first they are quite alike: eating, sleeping, pooping, crawling curiously about. Given the right conditions, both will become larger. But the cub is never going to become more bearlike, while the human child has the *potential* to become more and more (or less and less) human—to become like Joan of Arc and Thomas More or like Bonnie and Clyde. All bears are more or less alike, but there is a whole *spectrum* to the meaning of "human," ranging from Mother Teresa and Terry Anderson at the noblest extreme, down through ordinary folk like ourselves, to "inhuman humans" like mob hitmen, terrorists, and the pitiful dead-ended souls we see lying drunk or drugged on city streets. To *be* human is not the same as to *act* humanly.

That invitation is rooted in the human soul. You are free to refuse it, and the daily newspapers indicate many people do: murderers, child-molesters, drive-by shootists, drug lords, pimps. But those who refuse—or even scorn—the invitation to activate their human potential, their souls, are not limited to such dramatic cases. There are also workers grimly enduring dull jobs only to get the paycheck, grinding numbly along for 50 weeks a year for a too-brief two-week vacation. Prisoners in "rehabilitation" centers corralled like animals, scheming for dominance like animals, herded from task to task like animals. Students tolerating the opportunity to learn, to open their horizons, as if it were an unjust sentence, drudging for five days and coming alive only for a part of the weekend.

"Is that all there is?"

Evolving a Human Soul

There are (at least) five processes needed to evolve a human soul—and we are not speaking of religion yet; that goes much further. Even nonbelievers must evolve their souls, just in order to be fully human beings, and many have.

- *Admitting* that, beyond the mind and body, one even *has* a soul, acknowledging that one's soul—one's humanity—is only a potential that need not be activated, and committing oneself to the effort to bring it into actuality. We have already cosidered that process.
- Activating the *imagination*—all the right brain human powers denied in Mr. Gradgrind's school and in the rationalist society based solely on "the empirical, this-wordly, secular, pragmatic, contractual, hedonistic, disenchanted."
- Developing a sense of the *numinous,* that is, a sense of the sacredness (again, not yet religious) of nature, what the ancients called the *anima mundi,* "the soul of the earth."
- Beginning to evolve a personal *philosophy of life,* the priorities which show what is essential to human life and what is superficial, a pattern which gives order, significance, and a sense of wholeness.
- Evolving a personally validated *conscience* which knows not only *that* a given act is generally considered immoral but *why* it is—and yielding to that truth.

Imagination

The right brain potential of the human mind is given short shrift in our schools. In a budget crunch, it is axiomatic that the first cuts must be to art and music so that the "real" subjects like math and science suffer no harm; even English becomes not an opportunity to *feel* and *experience* what the great writers have experienced, to "taste" the juice of an author's verbs, to feel wonder at the possibilities of human dignity and depravity, but rather to *analyze,* develop the SAT verbal skills, and pass objective tests. As Winston Churchill once wrote, "My education was interrupted only by my schooling." Learning has yielded to

SACRAMENTS: RITES OF PASSAGE   43

an arbitrary process which has nothing whatever to do with "real life," endured as the price of achieving work credentials, with no interest whatever in the common humanity and common environment all education's disciplines scrutinize—not to master but to understand. Gradgrind would be pleased.

And of course when schooling is over, there are far too many more "important" elements in life to engage our attention: work, bills, taxes, family squabbles, neighborhood problems, finicky automobiles. And of course mind-numbing television.

Little wonder we have a society as soul-less as the one pictured so grimly in the first chapter. The soul's instrument is the imagination. Unused, the imagination atrophies and dies, and with it the human soul.

Learn to sketch, write a story, make music rather than merely listening. Your soul will waken.

The Numinous

The word "ecology" comes from the Greek *oikos,* which means "home." We share life with everything on this planet; we share the *anima mundi.* Native Americans felt it profoundly. When the government wrote to Chief Seattle in 1852 with an offer to buy Indian land, he wrote back:

> The earth does not belong to man, man belongs to the earth. All things are connected like the blood that unites us all. Man did not weave the web of life, he is merely a strand in it. Whatever he does to the web, he does to himself.

Today when we sit down to eat, some of us thank God for the food; more primitive tribes prayed to thank the animal they hunted and that its spirit would return, as one would thank a friend for cooperating in a mutual relationship. For them, nature was not mute; it "spoke," I to Thou, not I to It.

Now in the jungles of our cities, as the asphalt spreads and the forests recede, we become tougher-souled. No one notices heaps of garbage, noise, old tires, rusty appliances, broken furniture, rusty cars, weeds, unless they are especially blatant. No one feels the smothering, soul-less rage that sprayed the graffiti. Rationalism, opportunism, enlightened self-interest have freed us from superstition, but we've lost our souls. We do not turn to devils but to anaesthesia. The Earth Mother is demythologized into nothing more than dirt, under which may lurk oil or uranium. We are so weakened by spiritual anemia that we have lost even our sense of evil.

Every soul needs a walk in the park at least once a week.

A Philosophy of Life

The psychiatrist Carl Jung wrote: "A sense of a wider meaning to one's existence is what raises a person beyond mere getting and spending. If they lack that sense, they are lost and miserable." Of course the primary concern of every human being is staying alive, and thus also the concern to secure what allows us to live: food, clothing, and shelter. But if that occupies our lives *exclusively* then, as Chief Seattle also wrote, it is "the end of living and the beginning of survival."

The root of people with character—as opposed to those to whom life's disjointed events merely "happen"—is that they have found at least a tentative answer to that most important and profound (and ironically seldom posed) question: What are people *for?* Or, to put that same question in other forms: What does "success" *really* mean? What does a totally fulfilled human being look like? What must I do, or have, or achieve to be happy?

We've been conditioned (brainwashed, actually) by the Economy through its agents the media to believe the key which unlocks all those questions is simple: money. One would doubt that many readers of these pages would quibble with that. But money (and the means to it) is, as we have seen, a reductionist answer to a quite complex question. Food, clothing, and shelter are indeed indispensible to human life and therefore essential to human fulfillment. But they needn't be filet mignon, Armani, and condominiums. Many who have had their share—and more—of those luxuries have overdosed. That doesn't mean those who have money can't be happy, but if they are happy it is not the money that caused it. What is the secret, then? What do people who "have it all" possess *within* themselves which allows them to be rich yet still buoyant, hopeful, generous, high on life?

Answer that question and you will have begun to have a personal philosophy of life, a soul. Once you uncover that secret, all your priorities will line up in order.

Conscience

When each of us is born, we are, as we saw, little different from animal cubs: what Freud called the Id. But sometime during our second year, we begin to develop muscle control and teeth—through no fault of our own, just in the natural way of things. Before that transition, that conversion from infancy to childhood, everything we did was acceptable—no matter how inconvenient. Wet the diaper, toss the pureed vegetables, in fact toss everything, and the parents clean it up; if you're inconvenienced, wail and it will be taken care of.

But once nature has given you the means to control yourself, at least in some measure, you begin to hear for the first time ever words you will hear in various forms thenceforth for rest of your life: "Good" and "Bad." That is when your parents begin taping on your innocent mind a Superego: a series of do's and don'ts you have no way to comprehend or critique but which you simply accept as the price of your parents' approval.

Then in the radical conversion of adolescence, when you finally have achieved a mental sophistication capable of dealing with Shakespeare and trigonometry, the nature of human development invites you to develop an Ego, your own personally validated conscience, to critique all those do's and don'ts and find which ones square with objective reality and which don't. But once again it is an invitation you can refuse, or ignore, or even be totally unaware of—as perhaps in most cases. Those who fail to rise to that challenge (like most people on situation comedies and the soaps) end up victims either of their taped Superegos or, rejecting those strictures, their own moody Ids. Or more likely living a life jerked around by both: "I really shouldn't do that . . . . But I *want* . . . . But . . . . Still . . . ."

It may seem out of place here, but analyze for a moment what makes a man or woman "sexy"? Isn't a major element of that quality the individual's (at least apparent) self-*confidence*—which makes that person enviable? The ironic result of passively adapting to others' needs, demands, goals (superego, boss, spouse, media, society) in order to secure their approval, or at least ward off their criticism, is that one ends up less valuable, less interesting, less desirable.

A Balanced Soul

The key to a healthy soul is seeing, affirming, and accepting the world *as it is* and not as we wish it were: good and bad, dark and light, the expectability of the unexpected. Wisdom begins when we come to peace with the unchangeable, which means surrendering all the self-defeating "if only's."

We also must beware of a reductionism in values, focusing our quest on the pursuit of any one virtue unbalanced by its opposite. Love, for instance, unchecked by hard-nosed common sense can devolve into enslavement; purity becomes prudery; devoutness turns into fanaticism; charity becomes gullibility.

As we have seen, the healthy soul has to have an openness to the activities and values of each semi-independent lobe of the brain; without that balance, we become coldly rational apes or sentimental dreamers; "There is no such thing as an unjust profit!" or "Nothing must stand in the way of love!" Unless the two radical powers of the mind have a healthy relationship, we end up acting half-wittedly.

Carl Jung established that the healthy soul is *androgynous,* that is, both masculine and feminine. It is a wedding of those "masculine" qualities associated with the left brain (and wrongly stereotyped to males): rationality, decisiveness, seeing values in a strict vertical line of importance, and those "feminine" qualities associated with the right brain (and wrongly stereotyped to females): intuition, inclusiveness, seeing problems in a horizontal plane which judges them not in isolation but in the context of other significant factors.

The masculine potential in a female, Jung called the *animus;* the feminine potential in a male, he called the *anima.* Note once again that they are powers which need not be activated—just as one's talent for football or dancing or the violin may be ignored, as can one's human soul. But we ignore them to the soul's peril: the male whose *anima* is completely dormant becomes a macho brute; the female whose *animus* is suppressed becomes a passive dormat. To be fully human, a male must not be afraid that tenderness, compassion, and compromise make him somehow effeminate, and a female must not fear that rationality, determination, and resolution make her somehow a kind of predatory "she-male." It's perfectly healthy for a man to weep when there is a reason, perfectly healthy for a woman to stand up and be heard.

It is interesting, however, that studies show men talk twice as often as women at public meetings, and twice as long when they do. Also males, of all ages, frequently jump into a discussion with objections before the speaker even makes clear what the proposition and arguments are, and females tend to sit quietly trying to understand before they question. Men more often want to "master" the data, the discussion, the situation; women more often want to find where the question is leading. The balanced male needs to learn to listen; the balanced female needs to learn to question.

The *animus/anima* is both a source of life wish in the soul (animation), but it can also be a source of death wish if it is neglected or denied (animosity).

The *animus,* the "man-within" a woman, is the invitation to initiative, courage, objectivity. But if it is suppressed and frustrated, it doesn't go away. It corrodes into the "shadow" side of the *animus:* obstinate, unbending, angry. Often she "projects" the suppressed masculine in herself onto some virile, unstoppable film star like Sylvester Stallone or Tom Cruise.

The *anima,* the "woman-within" a man, is the invitation to vulnerability, personal love, an openness to the nonrational (as opposed not only to the rational but the irrational). Suppressed and denied, the "feminine" in a man becomes shrewish, moody, making poisonous remarks. Often he "projects" the suppressed feminine in him onto idealized women like Marilyn Monroe.

The undeveloped *animus* needs to read *Joan of Arc* and see *My Fair Lady.* The undeveloped *anima* needs to read *A Separate Peace* and see *Ordinary People.*

Chapter Three

MEANING AND MYTH

Is there any meaning in my life that the inevitable death awaiting me cannot destroy?

—*Leo Tolstoy*

A Puzzlement

> If merely feeling good could decide the meaning of true happiness, drunkenness would be the supremely valid human experience.
>
> —William James,
> *Varieties of Religious Experience*

The Need for A Context

We have seen what losing one's soul—or never finding it—can do to a human life. At worst, the empty shell is a victim of obsessions, addictions, loss of purpose, frustrations, rages. Even in less dramatic cases, one prowls about in an emotional vacuum: emptiness, vague depression, meaningless busywork, disillusionment about family, a yearning for fulfillment. One high-school senior put it very well: "Why is fulfillment always in the *future?*" Excellent question. Perhaps the reason is that we look for fulfillment in all the wrong places.

So far we have seen the soul more or less exclusively in isolation: the single sovereign soul. But we also develop a sense of meaning from being *related* to what is *beyond* the limits of our own selves: parents, siblings, neighbors, fellow workers or fellow students, friends, our culture, and perhaps also the mysterious Beyond. They offer us a context, a background without which we are lost in some featureless Dali landscape. Even Didi and Gogo could not survive without one another.

Home

When a child wakes up in the night after a bad dream and finds herself alone in the dark, reality is all askew; she's lost in a dark landscape where there are no reassuring landmarks. So she cries out in terror for her mother, and her mother is there, turning on the light, holding the child in her arms, rocking her and saying, "Everything's okay, honey. Everything's just fine." Wordlessly the child accepts that *order* has been restored to her world, and things are "as they should be." All of us, no matter what our age, need some sense that "Everything's okay."

Home is a "sacred" place, even for the nonreligious. Just as religious people believe that, at the doorsill of a church, they step from secular space into sacred space, all of us believe there is a special space behind our own doorsills which simply cannot be violated. This is my place, where I can close the door on chaos and find some kind of cosmos, peace, belonging. "Home is," as Robert Frost said, "the place where, when you go there, there are objects in that home which are also 'holy': a box of letters, an old photograph album, objects and pictures on your desk that say, 'This is mine; here is a place I *belong.*' "

Christmas is a "sacred" time even for those who do not practice or believe in religion. It is "a time to go home," to *recapture* a meaningful past where—even without reference to the Holy Family—family made everything more or less "make sense." Thanksgiving and Christmas are the busiest times of the year for the airlines: "Gotta get home! It's Christmas!" And *without* family, Christmas can be the most soul-harrowing time of the year; Christmas is also the time of the most suicides. We remember. And we want to go back when things were "right."

"I'll Be Home for Christmas." The media capitalize on that for a fare-thee-well: shows where the father is stranded in a snow storm with presents for his kids; the mother is in a sanitarium and the father and kids stand outside looking up at her window; even McCauley Culkin stranded *Home Alone* at Christmas has an unobstructed shot straight to our hearts.

That yearning to recapture a meaningful past surfaces year after year after year (with no diminishment in audiences) in *Miracle on 34th Street,* where the tough-mindedness of a sophisticated little girl is softened into humanity by her belief in a real Santa Claus; *It's a Wonderful Life,* in which a family is saved by the intervention of an angel; *A Christmas Carol* where a soul-less old curmudgeon is saved from death-by-cynicism by ghosts from his past.

Interesting to note that they are all about *second chances,* conversions to a richer life, and they are not all just about family; in each case the heroine or hero is set free from rationalism or despair or misanthropy by a supernatural agent. At Christmas time it's not naive to think of the supernatural as possible. "If only" it were true. The question is whether that "if only" is genuinely impossible, or if our skepticism makes it only *seem* impossible.

But home is also the place we have to *leave.* In folktales, stories that societies have told over and over for thousands of years to explain growing up, the heroine or hero is forced to leave home and go on a perilous journey, or some displacement in the home (like a new wicked stepmother) has made "home" not the same source of reassurance it had always been. It is true also of the great myths and parables: *The Odyssey,* the Old Testament uprootings of Adam and Eve, Abraham and Sarah, Noah, Rachel, Moses, David, the New Testament calls of Jesus and the apostles and Paul, the missions of Buddha and Mohammed, the prodigal son.

Hansel and Gretel, for instance, says children sooner or later have to leave the nest and discover how to make their own way by using their wits. But that need to leave home is just as true of the great folktales of our own day, as we will see in more detail later: Dorothy in *The Wizard of Oz* and Luke Skywalker in the *Star Wars* trilogy. They mirror the polar tension each of us feels in our souls (not in our minds or bodies) between wanting to belong and wanting to establish an independent self.

Yet even if the journey lies *away* from home, the goal is always to *return* home. As Dorothy says when she clicks her red slippers, "There's *no* place like home." But she returns to Kansas not the dismissible girl who was always in the way; she is now becoming a woman. The goal is to bring cosmos out of chaos again, but it will not be the old order but a new, different, better one.

The Numinous

As we saw briefly before, nature is also part of the background context in which we orient ourselves as selves. The ecology—*Oikos*—is also our "home," and the soul attuned to it can sense there, too, a sense of the "sacred," an intuition of the eternal within the temporal. The sensitized soul is aware of that "presence" on a summer-night sky strewn with stars, at the moment a woman first holds her child in her arms, or in the panic and relief of a nearly fatal accident. When we fall in love, places become "sacred," and only the time we are together is "really real." Compared to those privileged moments, all other times are dull and banal.

You do not *cause* those flashes of insight. You do not *make* an intuition; it comes to you. On the contrary, the presence of invisible power seizes the human subject, who is its "victim" and not its creator.

William James, the psychologist, writes:

> It is as if there were in the human consciousness a sense of a reality, a feeling of objective presence, a perception of what we may call 'something there,' more deep and more general than any of the special and particular senses.

The poet, James Russell Lowell, put it more accessibly:

> I remember the night, and almost the very spot on the hilltop, where my soul opened out, as it were, into the Infinite, and there was a rushing together of the two worlds, the inner and the outer . . . . I could not any more have doubted that He was there than that I was. Indeed, I felt myself to be, if possible, the less real of the two.

Until the disenchantments we saw in the first chapter—Protestantism, the Enlightenment, and the Economy, a sensitivity to that objective presence in nature was neither as difficult nor as rare as it seems to be today. Till societies were liberated from the enlivening uncertainties of the right brain, human beings felt more "at home" on this planet. There was a rhythmical "rightness" in the year resurrecting and renewing itself once again, in the reassuringly predictable sequence of childhood, adolescence, marriage, parenthood, old age, and death, in the patterned habits of the stars and planets. Now the stars are hidden by blankets of smog, flashing lights, and tall canyons made of skyscrapers. Now we merely . . . go on.

But it is still possible to experience that rush, for the soul restless enough to seek out its own enlivening.

The Culture

A rock is an intricate "society" of molecules older than any human one, so is the universe, so is the human body—all the disparate parts cohering into a single working whole: cosmos. A society of human beings would, ideally, work in the same way: each member finding his or her ideal place and purpose in helping the whole achieve fulfillment. That culture expresses itself and provides "directional signs" in the form of symbols: medals, feast days, rituals, which embody their beliefs about the purpose of human life, reward those who fulfill the common goals, unite the spirits of the individuals into the spirit of the whole through song, dance, prayer. But just as those "sacred" symbols unite "us" and give us a sense of cohesion, they also separate us from "them," those who are not "us."

In order to have power, then, symbols need a kind of "ghetto" in which we achieve a sense of unity not only by being together with a common purpose and symbols but also by being separated from "the others." In America in the 30s, for instance, Catholics had a sense of solidarity, no matter what their diverse ethnic backgrounds, by the fact that they had a Latin Mass, novenas, missions, benedictions, scapulars, Miraculous medals, fish on Friday, the body of Jesus on the crucifix (where fellow-Christian Protestants had an empty cross).

Further, even among Catholics in any given city there was a French church, a German church, an Irish church, a Polish church, an Italian church—all Catholic, yet each with its own customs, feast days, and practices brought from the old countries, which gave them at one time that sense of belonging and being separated. Some—mostly older people—still try to keep those customs alive: the St. Anthony's Day festival, the St. Patrick's Day Parade, St. Olaf's Day, when people put on what seem to outsiders outlandish Old World costumes that separate the "sacred" from the dull secular and give the participants a felt realization that they are different and special.

The Chinese have New Year's parades with smoke and gongs and huffing dragons; orthodox Jews wear long black coats, black hats, yarmulkes, beards. Recently, some African-Americans have tried the same symbolic means from the mother country to establish a sense of identity and pride: dashikis, caps, jewelry. The key is the *mother* country: the person/place where everything once made sense, where "Everything's all right."

Granted that the culture's customs often had more than a whiff of superstition to them, those symbols somehow put a bit of "magic" into life.

Then World War II broke down the ghetto "walls." Men from Boston and Brooklyn and Dubuque left homes from which many had never traveled more than a few miles, were forced to put off a great deal of their separateness, don a common uniform, and fight for a common cause. They traveled halfway across the world to Rome, Paris, Australia, Iwo Jima. Women left the household to work in war plants. And for five years all America became a "ghetto" with a common enemy and a common sense of purpose. And the effect on our common symbols was exhilarating: uniforms gave men and women a surge of pride; families proudly hung service star flags in their windows for sons who were in the services; "The Star Spangled Banner" brought men surging to their feet, unabashed for the tears in their eyes.

Then for a few more years it continued, in what we didn't realize at the time was our Golden Age. The economy was flourishing; people who had never heard of it were now eating pizza and "sending out for Chinese." We were (more or less) one, happy, contented family, at *home* in America. The avuncular Eisenhower gave us a sense we had a Grandpa who was serenely in charge, then the charismatic Kennedy embodied—symbolized—all that was good about all of us: young, handsome, funny, intelligent, confident.

Then on a day in November 1963 that symbol—and our idealism—was shattered by a bullet fired by a pasty-faced nobody, who in turn was shot by a strip-joint operator. It was obscene. And then the sorrows and disillusionments began to come in battalions: Bobby Kennedy, Martin Luther King, Vietnam, Kent State, Watergate, a president and vice president retiring in disgrace, drugs, street crime, wholesale divorce and abortion. As William Butler Yeats had written:

> Things fall apart; the centre cannot hold;
> Mere anarchy is loosed upon the world,
> The blood-dimmed tide is loosed, and everywhere
> The ceremony of innocence is drowned;
> The best lack all conviction, while the worst
> Are full of passionate intensity.
> —*The Second Coming*

Mass literacy, the explosion of knowledge, mass communication, and mass mobility slowly destroyed the unifying ghetto: America, the Church, the ethnic enclaves, even the family. Religious institutions, traditions, and symbols used to have a near monopoly on guiding thought, values, actions, on giving meaningful security to the soul. Now modern technological society has produced a territory "liberated" from the ties of religion. Business is business, and the sacred stops at the factory gate and the door of the office. If religion enters politics it is mostly rhetoric.

In a very real sense, you can find the "soul" of a culture—the drive which gives meaning, focus, and purpose to each of its members within their mutual association—by its tallest building. The teepee of the chief and the totem joining earth and sky was at the center of the village. The cathedral, rooted in the earth and pointing its steeples skyward, showed where the heart of the city and the people was. Today in the focal centers of our society the central building is the skyscraper—and not one unifying building but a host of them at odds with one another. On Fifth Avenue in New York City, St. Patrick's Cathedral, large as it is, seems a pitiably small building in contrast to the ones across the street: Rockefeller Center. The skyscraper is a good symbol for our culture—our home: upward mobility, getting to the top, progress, more, and there will never be an ultimately "tallest." We struggle away from nature to a top that isn't there. There is always more. The Tower of Babel is forever unfinished.

Now, home is a haven, a barrier *against* the culture, a place of sanity in which to hide. But the culture leaks electronically into our living rooms hour after hour. And the home is no longer the *oikos* we presumed it would always be. Job advancement calls for moves to other cities, other neighborhoods, new but unfamiliar landmarks. Now as never before there are different homes, different schools, different fathers. How does one forge a compass when everything we thought was reassuring becomes relative, changeable, uncertain? When the earth is hard as iron, and our compasses run wild?

It is interesting to compare what happened when the disenchanted-rationalist-utilitarian ethic took over from the credulous-homespun-altruistic ethic, which united us as recently as in our own grandparents' time, with what happened when "civilization" intruded on "primitive" societies in North America, South America, Africa, China, and Japan. Before that intrusion, they had what seemed to Europeans "primitive" social structures, although many of them antedated any European ideas. Not only did the invaders bring new ways and new gadgets (and new diseases), but they brought a scorn for the natives' beliefs.

Gradually, the original Americans were herded off workable land and out into the featureless wilderness; African medicine men refused to ply their trade because the white medicine men had "all the answers"; the original owners traded their sacred crafts for whiskey and wampum, which offered a much more reliable payoff than prayers to the gods. Gradually, that original society—with all its landmarks, all its validations of effort, all its purposefulness—disintegrated and died. What has Willy Loman done to Shane; what has Donald Trump done to Davy Crockett; what has Exxon done to Odysseus?

There are a few of us left who refuse to settle for so little. Care to join us?

Myth

The word "myth" has two valid but contradictory meanings, as different as "false" and "true." In its more common usage, it means a long and widely held delusion, as in "The Vietnam War dispelled the myth that America could never lose a war." The other, opposite meaning—as in the myths of Sisyphus, Eros and

Psyche, or Hercules—is a story which acts like a symbol, trying to capture a truth of human life in a right brain metaphorical way rather than in a left brain philosophical way. These systems of stories have been told and retold for thousands of years, passing from one culture to another so often that the details which individuate them to a particular culture erode, and what is left is a scheme embodying a *universal* truth, applicable to any human being of whatever time or culture.

Cro-Magnons 30,000 years ago had the same bodies and organs as we do today, which put the same demands on those primitives as they do on us: food, sleep, health, warmth, shelter. What's more, those earliest humans went through the same predictable but challenging physical and psychological stages as we do today: birth, infancy, childhood, learning the skills to survive and the customs of the tribe, puberty, parenthood, aging, and death. And the people of every culture between Cro-Magnons and people today have had the same human bodies and the same stages of human growth: Egyptians, Polynesians, Iroquois. Whether we lived in a cave in southern France or live in an apartment in New York, no matter how brutal or sophisticated our surroundings, we still have the same bodies and the same stages of human development.

Therefore, we respond to the same images, symbols, and stories every human being for 30,000 years has found helpful in order to understand those physical and psychological changes—what Carl Jung called "archetypes"—universal ideas grounded in the changes of the human body. Despite differences in hairiness, posture, food, weapons, dwelling places, every human story is the same story: birth, infancy, childhood, play years, learning years, adolescence, marriage, parenthood, aging, and death. As Joseph Campbell says, it's the same play but translated into different languages by different players. The story hasn't changed since the first *homo sapiens* lifted himself off his knuckles, looked around at the world, and asked "Why?"

Star Wars

Bill Moyers asked his son why he had gone back to see *Star Wars* a dozen times, and the boy answered, "Same reason you read the Bible all the time."

The message of *Star Wars,* though the ordinary viewer may not ponder it, is the same message this book has been stressing: technology is not going to serve us or "save" us. We have to rely on our intuitions, integrity, and courage. Luke Skywalker's life (as all of our lives) was a journey of self-discovery, the search for the challenges from which we wrest character, self-esteem, and dignity and which give us the wisdom and confidence to serve and protect others.

What follows is a dialogue between Moyers and the mythologist, Joseph Campbell, aired on PBS and published in the book *The Power of Myth* (Doubleday, 1988).

> MOYERS: Do you think, for example, that a movie like *Star Wars* fills some of that need for a model of the hero?
>
> CAMPBELL: I've heard youngsters use some of [director] George Lucas's terms—"the Force" and "the dark side." So it must be hitting somewhere. A good sound teaching, I would say.
>
> MOYERS: I think that explains in part the success of *Star Wars.* It wasn't just the production value that

made that such an exciting film to watch, it
was that it came along at a time when people
needed to see in recognizable images the clash
of good and evil. They needed to be reminded
of idealism, to see a romance based upon self-
lessness rather than selfishness.

CAMPBELL: The fact that the evil power is not identified
with any specific nation on this earth means
you've got an abstract power, which represents a principle, not a specific historical
situation. The story has to do with an
operation of principles, not of this nation
against that. The monster masks that are put
on people in *Star Wars* represent the real
monster force in the modern world. When
the mask of Darth Vader is removed, you see
an unformed man, one who has not
developed as a human individual. What you
see is a strange and pitiful sort of undifferen-
tiated face.

MOYERS: What's the significance of that?

CAMPBELL: Darth Vader has not developed his own
humanity. He's a robot. He's a bureaucrat,
living not in terms of himself but in terms of
an imposed system. This is the threat to our
lives that we all face today. Is the system going
to flatten you out and deny you your
humanity, or are you going to be able to make
use of the system to the attainment of human
purposes? How do you relate to the system so
that you are not compulsively serving it? It

doesn't help to try to change it to accord with your system of thought. The momentum of history behind it is too great for anything really significant to evolve from that kind of action. The thing to do is learn to live in your period of history as a human being. That's something else, and it can be done.

MOYERS: By doing what?

CAMPBELL: By holding to your own ideals for yourself and, like Luke Skywalker, rejecting the system's impersonal claims on you.

MOYERS: When I took our two sons to see *Star Wars,* they did the same thing the audience did at that moment when the voice of Ben Kenobi says to Skywalker in the climactic moment of the last fight, "Turn off your computer, turn off your machine and do it yourself, follow your feelings, trust your feelings." And when he did, he achieved success, and the audience broke out into applause.

CAMPBELL: Well, you see, that movie communicates. It is in a language that talks to young people, and that's what counts. It asks, Are you going to be a person of heart and humanity—because that's where the life is, from the heart—or are you going to do whatever seems to be required of you by what might be called "intentional power"? When Ben Kenobi says, "May the Force be with you," he's speaking of the power and energy of life, not of programmed political intentions.

MOYERS: I was intrigued by the definition of the Force. Ben Kenobi says, "The Force is an energy field created by all living things.[1] It surrounds us, it penetrates us, it binds the galaxy together." And I've read in *The Hero with a Thousand Faces* similar descriptions . . . of the sacred place, of the power that is at the moment of creation.

CAMPBELL: Yes, of course, the Force moves from within. But the force of the Empire is based on an intention to overcome and master. *Star Wars* is not a simple morality play, it has to do with the powers of life as they are either fulfilled or broken and suppressed through the action of man.

MOYERS: The first time I saw *Star Wars,* I thought, "This is a very old story in a very new costume." The story of the young man called to adventure, the hero going out facing trials and ordeals, and coming back after his victory with a boon for the community. . . .

CAMPBELL: Certainly Lucas was using standard mythological figures. The old man as the adviser made me think of a Japanese sword master. I've known some of those people, and Ben Kenobi has a bit of their character.

MOYERS: What does the sword master do?

CAMPBELL: He is a total expert in swordsmanship. The Oriental cultivation of the martial arts goes beyond anything I've ever encountered in

1. "The Force" is what we have seen before as the *anima mundi.*

American gymnasiums. There is a psychological
as well as physiological technique that go together there. This character in *Star Wars* has
that quality.

The Wizard of Oz

The same story is told from a girl's perspective in the undyingly
popular film *The Wizard of Oz,* which came out at the end of the
Depression, when Europe was already at war and America was
teetering on the brink of it. As Moyers says, "it came along at a
time when people needed to see in recognizable images the clash
of good and evil," a need for hope—and friends—in the midst
of despair. Hollywood, "The Dream Factory," has always been
able to reflect America's daydreams, and a myth is for a society
what a dream is for an individual: a way of symbolically
explaining what troubles us. Most of *The Wizard of Oz* is, in fact,
a dream, and like all dreams it contains the residue of Dorothy's
day before the cyclone hit: Miss Gulch who has taken Toto
reappears as the Wicked Witch, the three farmhands as the Tin
Man, Lion, and Scarecrow, and Dr. Marvel as the Wizard.

The story is a myth of a young girl forced (by the cyclone) to
leave home and go out on her own, and it deals with the two
questions which have bedeviled every adolescent for the last
30,000 years: Who am I? and Where do I fit in? Before, Dorothy
had moped around the farm, getting in everybody's way,
dreaming of an ideal world somewhere "Over the Rainbow."
She's an orphan (no explanation why), and the strongest figure in
her life is Auntie Em, a no-nonsense hardworking lady. Most of
the males in the black-and-white story which bookends the

dream are nice but ineffectual: Uncle Henry, the three farmhands, Dr. Marvel. In order to be a woman, does Dorothy have to be like Auntie Em?

Then as the technicolor dream begins and Dorothy finds herself "over the rainbow" in Munchkin Land, she's immediately hailed as a heroine for she has inadvertently killed a wicked witch. As a reward, Glinda the good witch gives her the dead witch's red slippers. But why doesn't Glinda send her back to Kansas right away? The "power" is in the slippers, and she already has them. But Dorothy has to find her power for herself. On her way, she falls in with three new friends, who—just as Toto is a symbol for Dorothy's own frisky spunk—are symbols of her own lack of self-esteem based on not being intelligent enough, not capable of loving enough, not courageous enough. During their many adventures, as in *Star Wars,* it becomes clear that however beautiful the world over the rainbow might be, it is just like this world. The difference is that, in this dream world, it is very clear where the good and the evil are, not as in this world all deceptively "smeared together."

It is Toto (Dorothy's inquisitiveness and spunk) who causes Dorothy to throw water on the witch when she is trying to burn the dog, and it is Toto who unmasks the Wizard. Unlike the roaring projection who terrified the foursome before, he is just a fussy old man manipulating levers. But he is entirely unlike the wicked witches. "Oh," says Dorothy, "you're a very bad man!" But the Wizard answers, "Oh, no, my dear. I'm a very good man. I'm just a very bad wizard."

The answer is not magic but kindness and wits. By the time they arrive back at Emerald City with the witch's broomstick, the friends have already *proven* they had more than enough heart and brain and courage; all they had lacked was belief in themselves.

So the Wizard merely makes it official by giving them symbols that capture those inner realities: a heart shaped watch, a diploma, a medal. And the Wizard promises to take Dorothy back to Kansas in a big bag of hot air. But it's not a man, however wise or kind, who can get Dorothy "home." It is Glinda the Good who tells her she must get back to Kansas by clicking her red heels and saying three times, "There's no place like home."

When Dorothy returns—just as Psyche and Odysseus on their return from the underworld—she is changed. She has brought home a self she can be proud of—a soul—energized by her adventures.

Leaving Home to Find Home

Why did Bill Moyers' son see *Star Wars* so often? "Same reason you read the Bible all the time." Study the themes of the Bible: creation, journeys and trials, death, resurrection, ascension, glorification, you will find the same basic stories in the myths of Egypt, Greece, Buddhism, Native American religion, the Arthurian legends, and all the myth systems the world over since the rise of human beings on this planet. At the bottom of the dark abyss (hell, underworld, forest, depths of the sea) is the light of salvation (one's hard-won soul, meaning, purpose, justification). The bleakest moment is the moment when transformation—conversion—comes. Surely the crucifixion of Christ manifests that truth, too.

There must be some reason for the basic similarity despite the different symbols chosen; for instance, the Tree of Knowledge of Good and Evil and the legend of the Fountain of Youth are both embodying the same human truth, but with different

symbols. The key is that myths are clues to the spiritual poten-
tialities of human life, no matter in what time or what culture.
They serve not so much to give an understanding of life as to
embody the *experience* of *being* truly, humanly alive! They give
inner sustenance in crises, making them bearable. They give
models of endurance, like Luke and Dorothy.

Stories of the call to leave home on a questing journey are so
constant in the stories of every culture in human history that that
call must be a universal in human spiritual growth. The hero or
heroine is one who gives his or her life to something bigger than
themselves and is ennobled by it. The journey is always a "death"
and rebirth, as it is captured perfectly in the heroic act of a
mother's labor and giving birth: risking her own life that a new
life might emerge. The Chinese *Tao Te Ching* says the same:
"When you have been hollowed out, you will be full." The
passion, crucifixion, and resurrection of Jesus says it too.

It is a journey which—to find a soul—we all must take.

Chapter Four

THE SUPERNATURAL SELF

What is that which gleams
through me and smites my
heart without wounding it?
I am both ashudder and aglow.
Ashudder insofar as I am unlike it,
aglow insofar as I am like it.

—*St. Augustine*

A Puzzlement

Speaking of Herman Melville's novel, *Moby Dick,* in which an obsessed sea captain named Ahab is in pursuit of a white whale which has maimed him and torn off his leg, the British journalist Bernard Levin writes:

The whale itself, perhaps the most gigantic symbol in all literature (it is a white whale, remember) no less certainly represents something greater than the greatest of sea beasts. Probably Moby Dick meant to Melville what the Hound of Heaven meant to Francis Thompson ("I fled Him down the nights and down the days"), for surely the whale is pursuing Ahab even as Ahab is pursuing the whale.

—The Listener, 12 August 82

The Beyond in Our Midst

Frequently in these pages we have considered our encounters with the numinous, the "sacred" in nature—the summer sky at night, the crackling thunderstorm, the vastness of the sea, the immensity of the universe, the sudden felt-awareness of one's own inevitable death and therefore of the preciousness of everything. It provokes in us the kind of awe the Lilliputians must have felt when Gulliver arrived. All along, cocooned in the everyday, they had thought themselves rather substantial personages. Then of a sudden this enormity shows up to humble their pretentiousness.

Now is perhaps the right time to take the quotation marks away from the word "sacred." Because the awe we feel in those encounters with the numinous—those moments when we say,

"Oh, my *God!*"—truly are encounters with God. They are moments of ecstasy—*ekstasis*—when we "stand outside" the everyday, and even outside of ourselves. A flash of eternity in the present.

> The world is charged with the grandeur of God.
> It will flame out, like shining from shook foil;
> It gathers to a greatness, like the ooze of oil
> Crushed. Why do men then now not reck his
>   rod?[1]
> Generations have trod, have trod, have trod;
> And all is seared with trade; bleared, smeared
>   with toil;
> And wears man's smudge and shares man's
>   smell: the soil
> Is bare now, nor can foot feel, being shod.
> And for all this, nature is never spent;
> There lives a freshness deep down things;
>   and though the last lights off the black
>   West went
> Oh, morning, at the brown brink eastward,
>   springs—
> Because the Holy Ghost over the bent
> World broods with warm breast and with ah!
>   bright wings.
>   —Gerard Manley Hopkins, S.J.
>   *God's Grandeur*

There is a genuine difference in our encounters with the "sublime," as in a first viewing of the Sistine Ceiling, and our encounters with the numinous in nature, as with the star-strewn

---

1. Respect his expectations of us.

sky. The awe we feel at seeing the Sistine Ceiling is a tribute to the artist, Michelangelo. The awe we feel at seeing the "firefolk sitting in the air" is—whether we are aware of it or not—a tribute to the Creator.

To clarify a few words we often use—or at least hear—and believe we vaguely understand: "sacred," "holy," and "supernatural." The word "sacred" does not mean merely "set aside from the secular" or "precious." It means "holy." And "holy" does not mean "completely good," in the moral sense of being "sinless, unblemished, faultless." It is, in fact, the presence of the transcendent—the supernatural—*in* our immanent world, what Dietrich Bonhoeffer called "the Beyond in our midst." Pictures we see in church, cartoons about people in heaven, perhaps even religion classes, have led us to believe—wrongly—that "supernatural" means physically *above,* as in "superstructure" or "supervise": above the clouds, "over the rainbow." Rather it means highly intensified, as in "supercharged" or "a superhuman feat," an infusion of aliveness from the Beyond, from another dimension of being real, which permeates and enlivens *the nature which was already there.* In fact that supernatural infusion—grace—does make us truly "superhuman."

The premise of the profane world, as we saw in the first chapter, is that no one who uses electrical appliances and computers and x-ray machines can believe in a dimension of reality that defies computation, left brain dissection, rigid scientific analysis. Yet those very valuable instruments of the mind are also incapable of coping with love, honor, dignity, dreams—which are nonetheless not only real but very important elements of fully human life. Such an inflexible reductionist stance does, in fact, place limits on what we *allow* to be real.

What's more, we've known since 1932, when Heisenberg won the Nobel Prize, that even the models of *physics* are no more than approximate *metaphors* (right brain) for realities we can't see. As Jung wrote, "It is almost ridiculous prejudice to assume existence can be only physical." Conflicting *ideas* have killed more people in the course of history than bubonic plague. And in the end, the secular world's denial of the supernatural becomes the triumph of the trivial, since all the medals, profits, condominiums, and skyscrapers shrivel into Lilliputian perspective in the face of the ultimate Gulliver, Death.

In a previous chapter we saw that money was no guarantee of happiness, fulfillment, success—since so many people had king's ransoms of money, yet overdosed. So if some wealthy people *are* happy, what do they possess *within* themselves which allows them to be rich yet still buoyant, hopeful, generous, high on life? When we've gone beyond all needs—beyond food, clothing and shelter, the need to belong, money, fame, sex, power, we find human beings are at the very core (potentially) religious beings, that there is no wholeness in us till we make the spiritual hunger more important than all the others. Perhaps the genuinely happy wealthy do not call that dominant inner need "spiritual hunger" or "soul." Perhaps they view it as "integrity" or "self-esteem" or "honor." But it is the same thing, just as awe at the numinous is a tribute to God, whether one realizes or not.

The sense of the sacred is no more irrational than sex is irrational. There is no way to explain either sacred or sex to someone who has not *experienced* them. It cannot be taught, only evoked, awakened—in the sense that "Buddha" means "the one who woke up." Nor is imagination at odds with knowledge. It is indeed a way of *illuminating* facts. But insights through imagination will be more ambiguous, more open-ended than strict formulas and definitions. When asked what a dance meant, the great choreographer Martha Graham said: "Mean? Darlings, if I could *tell* you, I wouldn't have *danced* it!" If you want to "understand" Handel's *Messiah,* I don't hand you the score. If you want to know why fans love baseball, it will be of little help to study the physics and geometry of the game. In all those cases—and in the case of the sacred—you have to experience them. And you have to develop a sensitivity to it, to evolve the *potential* within you, in order to apprehend the holy.

That experience of God is often lost in theologizing: studying *others'* experience of the numinous, as in the scriptures of any religion, only with left brain analysis and formulas. Thus, for instance, sacraments become merely conduits by which grace is "put into" us, like gas into a car, and quite often we feel no different for the experience. Rather, they are—or are intended to be—vulnerable *connections* to the Energy that enlivens all reality. If you want to understand the sacraments, you have to be as vulnerable to them as Martha Graham's audience to her movements and the fans to the baseball game. If you want really to *understand* God, I don't hand you a catechism. A book like this one may intrigue you to make yourself vulnerable to experience God, but it is no substitute for the experience.

It is difficult to deal with an entity like God, infinite and everywhere, immanent yet transcendent, real but unseen. And yet, surprising as it might be, most of reality around us we do *not* see, not just in the endless depths of the universe, but even in our very own rooms. We don't see other's thoughts, their lunches digesting, the blood pumping through their bodies, their fears, their hopes, their dreams. We don't see them, yet they are real. And very important. We don't see the alpha rays, gamma rays, muons and gluons and quarks whizzing all round us. We don't see most of the light spectrum, and yet it's there. We don't see the television and radio signals pulsing all around us. Yet they're real. We don't see the air, yet it keeps us alive.

Science says there can be no reality faster than light. Yet science also delights in playing "what if": what if we could make a medicine out of this bread mold; what if we could do something with these useless silicon chips? Well, what if there *were* a light, an energy, faster than light? It would be moving so fast that it would be everywhere at once. Like God. So dynamic that it would also be utterly at rest. Like God. And science now believes when it cracks open the last building block of matter it will find is nonextended energy. Like God. $E = mc^2$ means matter *is* energy. There is an insight there.

Couple that modern insight with the insight of Exodus. When Moses asked Yahweh his name, he was asking for much more than a label. For a Hebrew, one's name designated his or her role in the community. And God's reply was "I am who am." What is God's role in the community? Existence. God is the pool of existence out of which anything that *is* gets its "is." At least in that sense, insofar as the power of God is immanent, God *is* the *anima mundi*. When we react in awe and reverence to the numinous in nature, we are reacting to the Source of its aliveness and energy: "The world is *charged* with the grandeur of God."

The philosopher Thales of Miletus said that "Everything is full of gods." All round us, if we are aware, we find rumors of God. The epistle to the Hebrews says, "Remember to welcome strangers. . . . There were some who did that and welcomed angels without knowing it" (13:3). Anyone we meet on the street could be Obiwan Kenobi or Glinda the Good, sent as messengers, signals of God's presence in the world. Finding them (much less following them) depends primarily on our *openness* in our perceptions of reality. But it depends also on overcoming *TRIVIALITY*—and even before that *recognizing* that much of what we think really important is, against the background of the transcendent and Death, actually trivial.

How can we be sure our perceptions of the Beyond in our midst are not self-deceptions? The answer is simple: we can't, any more than we can be certain of the other discoveries of the intuitive right brain—love, faith, hunches. But just as the undeniable hungers to find answers and to survive death argue to a God who can fulfill them, Peter Berger in his book *A Rumor of Angels* (Doubleday, 1970) argues for several signals within human beings, of all times and cultures, that validate our apprehensions of the Beyond in our midst.

First, the argument from the inner human need for *order*, for the "mother" to come in at night and assure us "Everything's all right," not just within this home, but everywhere. But if the supernatural is a delusion, and all we have are a time-space reality, then what the mother lets her child believe is a lie: there is sickness "out there," dopers, DWI's, child abusers. If Freud is right, religion—the mother—is a fantasy that a Parent God will "make everything right." Ultimately (in the face of death) life makes no sense if this life is the *only* reality and not just a foreground of another transcendent reality in which love and suffering are not annihilated by death.

Second, the argument from the inner human need for *play*. Play sets up its own universe. In the "serious world," it may be 2:34 p.m., June 15, 1995, but in that world of play it is the third quarter, the second act, the fifth round. In that world there are no death and taxes. There is a "sacred immunity" here. It is the moment when Thomas More makes a joke to his hangman, when a band plays on the deck of *The Titanic:* acts of faith that this reality is not really as important as it seems.

Third, the argument from the inner human need for *hope.* We *count* on the future, even when things look impossible, as we see in courage in the face of death, getting married, having children. They are all death-defying, self-defying, rationalism-defying, cynicism-defying. It is rooted deeply somewhere within us to say "NO!" to death. Freud considered that also a childish self-delusion. But why are we the only ones who have it? Animals can recoil from danger, but we have no evidence they anticipate the reality of death and yearn to outwit it.

Fourth, the argument from the inner human need for *damnation.* That might sound somewhat sinister, as opposed to the inner need for salvation. But there is something ineradicable in us that demands a fitting punishment for deeds monstrous beyond the imagination, like the despicably casual indifference to the sacredness of human life and death in Nazi extermination camps. There must be justice. And even death is not punishment enough.

Finally, the argument from the inner human need for *humor.* We are not merely *animal rationale;* we are also *animal risible,* "the animal who laughs." There's *got* to be something more than Gradgrind! There's got to be something more than Didi and Gogo boring one another toward death and Gregor Samsa worrying about missing a train, despite the fact he is now a gigantic cockroach.

The very depth of their seriousness demands that we dance!

The *Mysterium Tremendum*

In his book, *The Idea of the Holy* (Oxford, 1923), Rudolf Otto calls that experience a contact with the *Mysterium Tremendum,* "the overwhelming mystery." It is a sense of awe at something objective, really-there, outside myself, which causes an involuntary feeling of smallness. When Abraham dares to plead with God for the citizens of Sodom (Genesis 18:27), his instinctive reaction is to doubt his worthiness: "I am bold indeed to speak like this to my lord, I who am but dust and ashes.". After the miraculous draught of fishes (Luke 5:8) when Peter begins to have some dim insight into an awesome power in Jesus, he says, "Go away from me, Lord! I am a sinful man!"

This response is not the same as being "humiliated," as by a bully, but rather in the sense of being "humbled," as by unexpected love. One has the sense (not a concept) of being so small in the face of something so powerful and enormous. We feel, at one and the same time, submissive yet elated. "Ashudder insofar as I am unlike it, aglow insofar as I *am* like it."

Mysterium

A mystery is always "beyond words," not because it cannot be understood, but one can understand it only by going through the process oneself. Puberty, for instance, is a reality one simply can't explain satisfactorily in words to a ten-year-old. Herman Hesse's Siddhartha found he had to leave the Buddha, because wisdom cannot come from listening to words about someone else's wisdom but only in *contemplation*. The same is true of comprehending the reality of the holy—not just as an external *rite* but as a felt experience.

Tremendum

The root of the word is *tremens,* "quivering," not from fear but from astonishment. Nor is it the same as "eerie, weird, dreadful," as listening to stories of ghosts or demons. It is, rather, awe. Today, we overwork the word "awesome"; now it means nothing more than "rather good." But it really means "breathtaking, wondrous, in-*spirit*-ing." This is fear only in the sense of fear before stored-up Energy, daunting and yet fascinating, intoxicating, urgent, compelling, alive. Humbling and exalting at the same time, honored for the privilege. At such moments we have come in contact with the living God rather than merely with the *idea* of God. *This is the root of all religion.*

When Abraham receives three shining Visitors (Genesis 18:3), he falls with his face touching the ground and says, "Please do not pass by my house without stopping: I am here to serve you." When Jacob emerges from a vision of God (Genesis 28:17), he is afraid and says, "What a terrifying place this is! It must be the house of God; it must be the gate that opens into heaven." When Moses encounters Yahweh speaking from within the burning bush, "He covered his face, because he was afraid to look at God" (Exodus 3:6). At his call to be a prophet (Isaiah 6:1), Isaiah has a vision of the Lord, "sitting on his throne, high and exalted," and he cries out, "What a wretched state I am in! I am lost, for I am a man of unclean lips and I live among a people of unclean lips" (Isaiah 6:5, The Jerusalem Bible). Not unclean in the sense of sinful but unworthiness in such a presence. Psalm 139:14 puts it well: "I praise you because you are to be feared; all you do is . . . wonderful."

In the New Testament, too, you find the same admixture of intimidation and exaltation in the presence of the truly holy.

When the Baptist speaks of Jesus (Mark 1:7), he says, "I am not good enough even to bend down and untie his sandals." When a centurion asks Jesus to heal his servant (Luke 7:6), he—a pagan—says, "Sir, I do not deserve to have you come into my house, neither do I consider myself worthy to come to you in person. Just give the order, and my servant will get well." At the transfiguration (Matthew 17:6–7), the divinity in Jesus burns through the limits of his flesh, and the three disciples see for an instant who he really is. "They were so terrified that they threw themselves face downward on the ground. But Jesus came to them and touched them. 'Get up,' he said. 'Don't be afraid!'"

Saul—who had held men's cloaks while they stoned the Christian, Stephen, and persecuted the renegade community— was walking along the road to Damascus to seek out and arrest the followers of Jesus when suddenly he was overwhelmed by a great light, and the voice of Jesus said, "Saul, Saul! Why do you persecute me?" (Acts 9:4). And in that moment, Saul was blinded for three days. But seeing that blinding light, he was converted, his whole life and way of seeing things turned around.

The Epistle to the Hebrews (10:31) captures the idea: "It is a terrifying thing to fall into the hands of the living God!"

This reaction to the presence of the holy is not reasoned but instinctive. Nor is it some kind of *moral* unworthiness because "I have done such and such sins." Rather it is a feeling of absolute profaneness in the presence of the holy, a sense of being "shadows in the Light."

It is not from our sins and sinfulness that Jesus came to ransom us, but from that sense of utter abasement, from that sense of unworthiness before God. Because the core of his message was that this *Mysterium Tremendum* is also our Father.

Salvation

It is difficult at a baptism to accept that, as the result of two not overly bright naked people eating *one* piece of fruit, this gurgling little bundle of new life, with perfect tiny fingers and beautiful eyes, who has yet to assume responsibility for her own excretion, is somehow "tainted" with original sin and thus "apart from God." That is a quite Protestant assessment of humanity as invincibly corrupted—even after baptism. What's more, it is a quite possibly blasphemous assessment of God, picturing God as blaming the entire human race, generation unto generation, for a single act for which they were not even alive to be aware of. It makes God a Dickensian judge herding an entire family, even innocent children, into debtors' prison for the mistakes of the father. If God were that vindictive, how to explain God's indefatigable solicitousness for wayward Israel in book after book of the Bible?

The economic metaphor springs too easily to mind when we hear the words "redemption, reparation, atonement," which associate the actions of God and Christ with the workings of pawnbrokers, process servers, and international tribunals after cessation of hostilities. Becoming locked in the inadequate metaphor, we turn God into a Banker, and not a kindly banker either; rather, one who refused to relent until every last shekel of the debt was paid in the blood of Jesus, who apparently nursed a grudge far longer than Jesus allowed us to. If we are about to sacrifice, Jesus says, and realize we still have a grudge against our neighbor, we should leave the offering on the altar and first go and become reconciled with our neighbor (Matthew 5:23).

And such an image of God goes directly counter to the image Jesus himself gave us in the father of the prodigal son (Luke

15:11–32). When the wayward boy headed for home, the father saw him while "he was still a long way from home," which means the father was out there every day looking for him. And the father "was filled with pity, and he ran, threw his arms around his son and kissed him"—*before* the boy even apologized! The father had probably forgiven his son before the boy was off the property, but his forgiveness couldn't be activated until the boy admitted he needed it. But *all* he had to do was come home! Even before the young man finished his memorized speech, the father interrupted him: "This son of mine was dead, but now he is alive!" And he didn't give him a retaliatory penance as "reparation" and "atonement," he gave him a party!

That is the picture of God Jesus gave us. Clearly not one who holds grudges, demands restitution, forgives "under certain conditions." God told us we must forgive 70 times seven times (Matthew 18:22), so we can expect at least as much from God. God is not just one for second chances; God is one for 490 chances!

As we saw in the first chapter, the Economy has become an unquestioned Idol, whose goals, values, and priorities dominate our own "personal" goals, values, and priorities. Thoroughly saturated as we are by economic metaphors and economic realities, unconditional forgiveness of debts seems at best simple-minded and at worst suicidal business practice. What would happen, for instance, if every 50 years every individual and nation forgave all outstanding debts? One more clear indication "God's ways are not our ways." But we can't impose our bruised feelings, our yearning for revenge, our reluctance to forgive on God's attitude toward weakness and failure, manifest in Jesus.

What, then, is original sin? Perhaps the cause was not a literal Adam and Eve, but nevertheless the effects of whatever-original-sin-is are undeniable. It is the only doctrine one can prove from the daily newspapers. While no other animal refuses to follow its instinctual programming, there is no doubt human beings refuse to act humanly. Nor is it merely the newsworthy who suffer from it. Within each one of us, there is a self-absorption which refuses to admit we've made a mistake, and an inertia which—even though we feel vaguely guilty—finds it too much effort to go back to the first wrong turn and start over. That "original sin" balks at conversion. Even saints like Paul were afflicted with it: "I do not understand what I do; for I don't do what I would like to do, but instead I do what I hate" (Romans 7:15).

One way to understand original sin—that inclination toward what harms ourselves and others—is to look at an old ape in a zoo. Unless he is irritated by something outside his smallish brain—hunger, intrusion, sexual urge, he will just lie there snoozing all day: self-absorption and inertia. Like it or not, he and I have the same ancestors. But he and I are also quite different; as far as we know, the old ape does not ask, "Why?" His dreams are untroubled by a realization that he will one day die. And he has no conscience to call him to task for failing to be more productive, losing his temper with his kids, swiping a few bananas from his neighbor's cage.

But I do. At least I have the *potential* to be more than a dumb brute: to be continually asking questions, reaching out to the helpless, conducting myself like a person of honor. But it is precisely the self-absorption and inertia I share with that old ape which too often holds me back. That is original sin. And despite the fact that little girl about to be baptized is not "sinful" or "apart from God," she does carry within her both the potential to be intensely more human than she is at that moment and the potential to atrophy as a human being. Baptism is an invitation to her—and perhaps more so to her parents and godparents—to encourage her continually to accept it.

"Salvation" is a value sought by *all* religions: redemption from a sense of meaninglessness, ultimate purposelessness, validation of one's suffering. It is too narrow to say Jesus died to "save us from sin," since his sacrifice did not eradicate my tendency to sin. And surely he did not offer himself up to save us from some future hell—which, like the economic metaphor for original sin, makes God want vindictive punishment.

Indeed, the Epistle to the Philippians shows God's response to the sacrifice of Calvary was not wiping out a debt but exaltation! (Philippians 2:9–11). Just as the father of the prodigal jubilantly welcomed his son back from his disgrace and bedecked him in the best garments and threw him a feast, the Father welcomes Jesus back to heaven to be glorified. And if God sent Jesus as a model for our lives, that is what God is preparing for each of us as well. Membership in the family of the Trinity. We are Peers of the Realm of God. That is what happens to the infant when she is baptized. She is welcomed "home" and glorified.

The "sin" which the sufferings of Christ atoned for was not merely eating a piece of fruit. It was not even to "wipe from God's mind" the enormities human beings have perpetrated against one another since the beginning—much less to wipe out the secret nastiness of which each of us has been guilty. It was to heal the *estrangement* between humankind and God, to welcome us "home."

We have had a better metaphor to understand what "original sin" and "salvation" mean all along, in the Covenant which Yahweh swore with Israel on Sinai, a marriage to which Yahweh (unlike a grudge-bearing God) was never unfaithful, yet which Israel deserted again and again. It is clearest in the book of the prophet Hosea, who says that the people are "like a woman who becomes a prostitute; they have given themselves to other gods" (4:12). But again and again Yahweh comes after that prostitute people, just as Jesus came to us, to heal the estrangement:

> So I am going to take her into the desert again; there I will win her back with words of love. I will give back to her the vineyards she had and make Trouble Valley a door of hope. She will respond to me there as she did when she was young, when she came from Egypt. Then once again she will call me her husband.
>
> *(Hosea 2:14–16)*

That image of God—so consistent with the image of the father of the prodigal—shows how sin and salvation are connected: forgiveness, for all those willing to avail themselves of it. Every one of the sacraments is precisely that: a second chance, welcoming "home," where everything is right again.

After his temptations in the desert, Jesus came to the Nazareth synagogue, opened the scroll of Isaiah and read:

> The Spirit of the Lord is upon me,
>   because he has chosen me
>   to bring good news to the poor.
> He has sent me to proclaim liberty to
>   the captives,
>   and recovery of sight to the blind,
>   to set free the oppressed
>   and announce that the time has come
>   when the Lord will save his people.
>
> *(Luke 4:18–19)*

That is Jesus' statement of purpose, his mission, the meaning of the "salvation" he brought us: good news, liberty, clear-sightedness, liberation from oppression. The final verse is better translated "to announce the Year of Grace," which is much clearer about what "when the Lord will save his people" means. That Jubilee Year, outlined in Leviticus 25:8–55, occurred every fiftieth year, when all debts were forgiven. It was the Year of the *Amnesty* of God: all is forgiven, no strings.

But first we have to admit that our idols, our Baals, have led us to poverty, captivity, blindness, oppression. Even God himself cannot grant us forgiveness and freedom until, like the prodigal, we admit we need them and head for home.

The initial question then is to ask ourselves what our "idols" are. The first chapter suggested a few.

Conversion

The process of conversion is a complete turnabout, a radical change in priorities, an admission—against the forces of original sin (self-absorption which refuses to admit mistakes and inertia which refuses to change)—that I need to take a completely fresh look at . . . everything. For instance, "I've bought the whole materialist idolatry, and it's empty, unfulfilling, delusional. What do I do now?"

One way is to consider the highly successful method of the so-called Twelve-Step programs, which began with Alcoholics Anonymous:

1. We admitted we were powerless over _____ and that our lives had become unmanageable.
2. Came to believe that a Power greater than ourselves could restore us to sanity.

3. Made a decision to turn our will and our lives over to the care of God *as we understand Him.*

4. Made a searching and fearless moral inventory of ourselves.

5. Admitted to God, to ourselves, and to another human being the exact nature of our wrongs.

6. Were entirely ready to have God remove all these defects of character.

7. Humbly asked Him to remove our shortcomings.

8. Made a list of all persons we had harmed and became willing to make amends to them all.

9. Made direct amends to such people whenever possible, except when to do so would injure them or others.

10. Continued to take personal inventory and when we were wrong, promptly admitted it.

11. Sought through prayer and meditation to improve our conscious contact with God *as we understood Him,* praying only for knowledge of His will for us and the power to carry that out.

12. Having had a spiritual awakening as a result of these steps, we try to carry this message to [sufferers] and to practice these principles in all our affairs.

The physical conversion of adolescence is out of our hands, like the emergence of a butterfly. But the psychic conversion of a child into an adult is an invitation we can refuse. So is the spiritual conversion from a life focused unflinchingly on buying and selling, beating the system, getting out of school, proving myself by one-upping everyone else, turning completely around to a concern for being a fully-realized human being. Even further, it is a major conversion to surrender my need to "control it all" to the One who truly controls it all.

Athletes may come to a point where all the bits and pieces, all the practice, no longer mean anything. They "lose themselves" in the game, and the game "plays itself," or rather the game plays itself *through* them. The same happens sometimes with musicians: when the music "plays them." So too with religious conversion: "It is no longer I who live, but it is Christ who lives in me" (Galatians 2:20).

It comes from ceasing to resist, to try to do it alone, letting the Larger Power surge up from within. The key is self-surrender: "Let go! I'll catch you!" Just as I stand, I am *accepted* by God. Acquiescence and assurance.

But it is not solely a matter of accepting God, or even of being accepted *by* God. It is also inviting that Power—and its power—into myself, into my life.

Grace

Grace is the aliveness—the power—of God in me, the indwelling of God; that *is* salvation. Jesus said, "I have come in order that you may have life—life in all its fullness" (John 10:10). It is God's will for us that, in Jesus Christ, we become not only fully human but *super*human, supernatural.

In *The Varieties of Religious Experience* (Longmans, Green, 1902), the psychologist William James wrote that the grace of God operates "through the subliminal door," through the intuitive potential of the undervalued right brain. Some of the effects of opening oneself to grace are: a feeling of being in a wider context than the world's selfish interests; a friendly continuity with an ideal Power and surrender to it; elation and freedom; a shifting of the emotional center to "Yes"; open-handedness, openheartedness, openmindedness.

As Clare Booth Luce asked, "Can I see your freedom? Can I feel your joy?" Anyone connected to the grace of God ought to be more graceful, more gracious, living more abundantly.

There are channels of grace everywhere, not only in nature and in the sacraments, but in people. When Hindus greet one another, they place their palms together (as they do when praying) at the center of their foreheads. That gesture "says" that the god in me bows to the god in you.

When Jesus speaks of the Last Judgment (Matthew 25), he says the one question that will determine whether the life you lived was worth it will not be how much money you made or how often your name was in the newspapers, nor how often you divorced or practiced birth control. There will be only one question:

"I was hungry, I was thirsty, I was imprisoned, I was lonely. What did you do about that?"

In *Sleep with the Angels* (Moyer Bell, 1994), Mary Fisher speaks of such graceful, grace-filled moments:

> This is grace: When your child tries and fails, and ruins your family name; when he tells you secrets you hope the neighbors never uncover; when he says, "I've been arrested," when she blurts out, "I had an abortion," when full of fear they, trembling, stammer, "I wanted to die. . . ." When at that moment neither pride nor reputation slow you down on your rush to lift them up, cradle them in your arms, kiss their tears and tell them you love them—this is love undeserved. Grace.
>
> This is grace: The high school senior was undergoing cancer therapy. On top of the crushing fear and daily nausea, he suffered the added indignity

of losing all his hair. Still, when the day came that the therapy ended, he headed back for school. When he walked through the door that first morning, there were all his friends with shining bald heads. They had, every one of them shaved their scalps clean. They could not take his cancer, but they could relieve his shame.

Grace is that same solicitousness, a self-communication of God to us, if we are willing to receive God. And as we will see more extensively later, each of the sacraments is a mutual vulnerability between God and ourselves, each one a conversion, each one a welcoming home. Baptism, of course, is the first welcoming. Reconciliation is the prodigal returning to the Father, to be welcomed—unconditionally—home. The eucharist is the meal which celebrates our at-homeness, an opening to the eternal each week, in which the false promise of Satan in the Garden comes true: "Eat this and you *will* become like God." At Confirmation we solemnize the beginning of the long conversion from childhood to adolescence, the process by which we learn the new role we have as adult members of the family. In marriage two people *become* a new home, an exchange of selves which is a conversion of two lives into one life, and a promise of new human and superhuman life. Holy Orders converts an individual from the service of the ordinary Christian to the service of the servants, to mediate the prayers of the people to God and the grace of God to the people. And the Anointing of the Sick puts life and death before that far larger background of the eternal so that we can see death as it really is: a welcoming home.

Chapter Five

SYMBOLIC RITUALS

What is essential is always invisible.
—Antoine de Saint-Exupéry

A Puzzlement

There is a sacred Hindu adage that says: It is a holy thing to clean a toilet very well.

Symbols

In trying to understand the world and ourselves better, the mind has at hand two quite different functions of the brain: the left lobe deals primarily in clear-cut rational definitions, the right lobe deals primarily in less precise but often more illuminating symbols. The meticulously rational dictionary takes 42 finely printed lines to define "love," and at the end one understands little more about real loving than if the definition had been printed in Mandarin. On the other hand, a little girl's carefully cornrowed hair or a little boy spruced up in Sunday best "says" love, too, and a lot better than 42 lines of prose.

Definitions best isolate realities which are cut-and-dried, literal, clearly-this-and-nothing-else: aardvark, electromagnetism, monarchy, cranium, zygote. Symbols suggest, rather than isolate, in order to provoke a better *understanding* of more elusive realities: love, loyalty, courage, justice, the spirit of a society. Similarly, although a carefully reasoned philosophical treatise gives us a clear skeletal *explanation* of, say, atheism, two hours watching the symbolic story of Didi and Gogo struggling to keep busy gives us a less clear but more profound *understanding* of what atheism really is, how it "feels." The stories of Luke Skywalker and Dorothy not only entertain but, like the stories in Bill Moyers' Bible, help us understand better what we must do in order to fulfill our humanity. Parables are like parabolas; they come at the truth "around the corner."

Again, it is important not to approach symbols with the literalism of the left brain. If someone says, "Let these roses show you how much I love you," the literalist has to say that when the roses wilt the love has died. If a pagan Australian bushman went into a European cathedral and looked around, he would come out saying, "These people worship a big white bird." If Jesus literally ascended "up" into heaven, even traveling at the speed of light, he'd still be inside the Milky Way galaxy.

We resort to symbols simply because there *are* realities— honor, the human soul, the afterlife, God—which truly exist but are not visible or physical. Yet we human beings are physical, and our ability to apprehend external realities begins in our physical senses. Even our experience of the numinous in nature begins with our eyes and ears and skin. As we saw before, no one really sees *you*—your real inner self, your soul—but only your body, and they can begin to understand you only *through* the actions and words of that body. Somehow, we want to understand the invisible-yet-real *as if* it were visible.

In H. G. Wells's story, "The Invisible Man," the hero discovers a way to make himself unseen, and in order to get into situations undetected, he has to go naked. But when he *wants* to be seen and communicate with someone, he has to put on an overcoat and hat and wrap his face in a bandage. That is what symbols do for ideas and nonphysical realities: wrap them up in "clothes" so that we can see them better. As Thomas Carlyle said, symbols are "the time-vesture of the eternal."

Like so many other words we've seen so far, the word "symbol" is often used slapdash—like the words "love, value, awesome." Companies use logos to isolate immediately their product as different from some other company's. After all the ads, each of us can tell the Cadillac "symbol" from Ford,

Volkswagen, Jeep. But those pictures—which immediately identify—are not strictly speaking symbols; rather, they are "signs," idea-pictures, which denote (separate from all others) rather than connote (suggest a value.) If a picture of a fish, for instance, means "Buy fish here," it is no more than a straightforward sign, a signal, a pictogram. But if a fish sign in a catacomb means "We are Christians," then it is a symbol. Not just a designation but a declaration of *values*.

To make the distinction clearer: Efficient mass production demanded a revolution in the art of selling: consumerist advertising, a shift from a rational style that focused on the product's demonstrable, objective *qualities* (a sign) to an emotional appeal to the consumer's psychological, subjective *needs* (a symbol). For instance, when Ford first brought out the Model-T, its advertising and salesmanship focused on the inherent value of the car itself: transportation, economy, ease of repair (a straightforward sign). But then the market became saturated; everybody who could afford one already *had* a Model-T which, as advertised, took a great deal of time to wear out; but who was going to buy the new ones coming off the assembly line? The advertisers and salespeople had to find a motivation for customers to want to buy a *new* Ford (even though the one they had was still good for years). So they began advertising a "newer, improved, better" car, "sleeker, more aerodynamic," and ultimately "sexier." The connotations surrounding cars no longer were principally objective (maintenance, mileage, durability) but rather the car was an *ego-enhancer*: freedom, mobility, sexual prowess, rising social status. You can see that difference in the gap between the dull "Model-T" and the muscular "Mustang."

Words are symbols, too, and they not only denote—"light, female parent, equine quadruped," but they also connote—

"moonbeam, Mom, steed." It is the connotations that give the words *power*—"*Sieg heil!*, a day of infamy, *Ich bin ein Berliner!*, I have a dream!, I absolve you from your sins; this is my Body." The words "he loves me" are verbally identical whether a girl uses them about her father or about her fiancé, but in each case "love" is qualitatively different. In the sacraments of marriage and reconciliation, the words *are* the sacrament.

Symbols are a means to convey not only an idea but the *value* of the idea, they are "charged," like a battery ready to deliver power when it is grounded in a ready receiver. A symbol is a channel which somehow "connects" the viewer with the power of the value. It is like an acorn unfolding itself into the roots and branches of a great oak, far bigger than its apparent self.

Much of what we say is not literal but figurative (without our even realizing): "I'm gonna kill you, you rat; she's got a brick for a heart; I came out of there walking six inches off the ground!" And in dealing with the transcendent—which is by definition not visible—we can only use symbols. Louis MacNeice said that a symbol is "a signature of God's immanence." Nathaniel Hawthorne wrote: "Everything has its spiritual meaning, which is to the literal meaning what the soul is to the body." And Walt Whitman: "Symbols are letters from God dropped in the street, and every one signed by God's name."

William James says in *The Varieties of Religious Experience:*

> What keeps religion going is something else than abstract definitions and systems of concatenated adjectives, and something different from faculties of theology and their professors. All these things are after-effects, secondary accretions upon those phenomena of vital conversation with the unseen divine.

On the one hand, we know that God is in a dimension of reality beyond the physicality of time and space; therefore, God is not male, does not sit on a throne or have hands or a voice. On the other hand, God is not some mere abstraction, like fidelity or mathematics or the Uncaused First Cause. Therefore, it helps us understand and deal with God if we act *as if* God were not everywhere but sitting right next to us in the passenger seat. Some combine the insights of science and Exodus into light helpful and think of God as "a Person made of light." And Jesus made it even easier, since the Son of the Invisible God did put on clothes to walk among us, to show us how to live and die well. But Jesus did not just "put on" humanity, like a tunic, he fused divinity into humanity so we could understand God better.

Natural vs. Culturally Conditioned

Symbols are words, objects, places, and actions which evoke more than their literal meaning: value. There are some symbols which evoke value simply by what they are, in any culture or society: natural symbols. Other words, objects, places, actions, evoke a particular value only within a particular culture.

Natural Symbols

Roses make us so readily think of fragility, beauty, and femininity, it is often easier to associate roses with women than with other vegetation. Birds call to mind freedom, in any culture, thus some other creature with wings suggests throwing off constraints: Icarus, Pegasus, Hermes with winged helmet and sandals, angels.

The phoenix rising from its ashes and a butterfly emerging from an ugly caterpillar are obvious symbols of resurrection and rebirth. In any culture, bread means food and wine means celebration. Primitive tribes fixed a totem pole carved with faces of their guardian animal spirits at the center of the village, the focus of the people, anchored in the earth and yet reaching up into the heavens; the same is true of the cross on Calvary, the medieval cathedral.

The midwinter and spring solstices are meaningful in all cultures. At midwinter the nights are longest, and the skies have been grey for weeks, saturating our souls with gloom and—no matter where we are—we yearn for a rebirth which seems so far away, so we remind ourselves of the rhythm of nature and celebrate the promise of new life on the darkest night of the year: in the Mithraic cults, the Day of the Unconquered Sun; in Christianity, Christmas. Then when spring begins to seem more than just a faint hope, we have Passover and the escape from Egypt, Easter and the resurrection, with eggs which are a natural symbol of birth and bunnies, the essence of fertility.

Though he was not of our culture, that young man standing in Tienanman Square, arms at his sides and head bowed before two gigantic tanks "says" dignity and courage under oppression to anyone, in any culture, and far better than any dictionary.

Our dreams (like Dorothy's) are filled with natural symbols, what Jung called "archetypes." A white boy dreams that he is an African bushman marauding a colony of white missionaries (his anger at his overly pious parents); a girl dreams her mother is backing the car out of the driveway in anger, and she runs after her through air like lucite, soundlessly crying, "Mommy!" (her fear that, no matter what she does, she can never get her mother's approval); a man who has no success with women dreams he is at the mouth of a cave whose floor is quicksand, one foot in and one foot out (his fear that if he becomes seriously involved with any woman she will be as devouring as his mother). Dreams are symbolic stories our unconscious tells us about ourselves.

Culturally Conditioned

Because of its shape—self-contained, whole, a surface around which anything could travel forever, and its association with the global earth and planets—a sphere is a natural symbol for perfection. But though you may know a horseshoe, a four-leaf clover, and a rabbit's foot are symbols of good luck, there is no way you could deduce that from their shape.

Some symbols have meaning only within a matrix hallowed by tradition and evoke a sense of value only in those who are aware of that tradition and revere it. An American flag is just a piece of cloth, but it has been made "sacred" by its association with our past: the revolution, the Civil War, Iwo Jima. The Liberty Bell is just a cracked antique; the Bill of Rights just a piece of paper ornately penned; voting seems an ineffectual act when there are so many other voters; Monticello is just a well-preserved old plantation. But not to those who cherish the tradition behind them. For them they radiate a very real value.

Similarly, clothes "speak." Why do judges wear robes and not just appear in pinstriped suits like the lawyers? Because the robe "says" authority. A Roman collar, a badge, a nurse's uniform do the same. A varsity jacket is nothing more than a coat, but within that small society it has been "charged" by a season of shared blood, sweat and tears. "Grunge" clothes make no statement at all unless the majority of the society wants button-down collars and long skirts. Ethnic costumes from "the old country"—kilts, pajamas, saris, dashikis, turbans—give a value and sense of identity only to those who revere them.

You might want to be married in the Navajo rite because the words are nice and the ritual very attuned to nature, but the rite itself will not make a Navajo marriage or suffuse your lives with the Navajo mysteries. Similarly, you may want to be married in a Catholic church or have your child baptized or your parents buried, but there is at least something "untoward" about making use of those symbolic rites when they have less meaning to you than choosing the bridesmaids' dresses, the music, and the limousine, when those are the only three occasions in your adult life you are ever in a church. That is like coming "home" only to "use the facilities."

Culturally conditioned symbols have meaning only for those who are "in on" the society's code. Apocalyptic books in the Bible (such as Ezekiel and Revelation) are filled with bizarre symbols like monsters with many horns and eyes, flying wheels, mammoth statues made of different materials. They were written during times of persecution as "underground" messages to give hope to the oppressed that the invaders would be defeated, using symbols meaningful only to them and not to the persecutors.

In 2 Maccabees, an old man named Eleazar was commanded to eat pork in public, but even when they offered him other food disguised as pork so he could save his life without violating his conscience, he refused, not to uphold only one law but the Law that gave his people an identity. A pinch of incense on smoldering coals would seem an insignificant act, but when the coals were at the feet of a statue of the "divine" emperor, that act took on an entirely different meaning for an early Christian. A signature is nothing more than a configuration of ink on a paper, but Thomas More refused to sign his name—which was his "word"—because signing meant far more than just lines on a page; it would symbolize his denial of the primacy of the papacy in religious matters.

Ritual

We need to *express* our beliefs, to externalize our private convictions, just as we need to express our love.

Something in us also hankers for ritual to break the deadening routine and put our lives into a bigger context. Games begin with the national anthem, and even if it carries no "sacredness" at most times, God help any corpulent comedienne who mocks it. When the Rangers won the Stanley Cup after 50 years, there *had* to be a parade. Without the fireworks, the Fourth of July would be just another day. The Olympics have to begin with the torch. No one wants to finish high school or college and just walk away; there has to be some kind of ceremony. There are three moments in life, even for people who "don't need church," when they definitely do need church: birth, marriage, and death, moments too *important* to be solemnized in some civil office.

Secular Rituals

The Democratic and Republican presidential campaigns are a whole series of ritual extravaganzas to elicit *belief* in the candidates: primaries, conventions, campaigns, culminating in the final ritual when the president is inaugurated. Decked out with balloons and bunting, orchestrated speeches and responses, past heroes trotted out, processions, noisemakers, signs. Election night, TV anchor people sit before electronic maps like Druid priests explaining where it's all going. And finally the inauguration takes place amid hymns like "Ruffles and Flourishes" and "Hail to the Chief," formal oaths, a rousing sermon on American values and purposes. It gives us a sense of being a democracy.

Sports, too, have their rituals, cathedrals, "sacred" objects. Trips to the Super Bowl, World Series, Olympics, and Final Four are what visits to Mecca are to Muslims and trips to Israel are to Jews and Christians. The stadiums are "holy" places set aside from the everyday, most of them bigger than the Roman Colosseum, temples to competition. The ritual begins with the national anthem, which makes it very "American," and there is often a goddess-queen. Costumed cheerleaders and bands act like acolytes and choirs. Mascots, like the idols of primitive tribes, embody the *spirit* of the team—Eagles, Rams, Buccaneers, Tigers. For each sport, there is a Pantheon, a Hall of Fame, where the great heroes are enshrined like Odysseus and Hercules. The game ball has a special meaning within the culture, and fans (from "fanatic") take home souvenirs like relics. Some follow the season as scrupulously as a liturgical calendar. But when the fans are at the game, they are out-of-the-ordinary, hyper-alive yet self-forgetful, "charged up." People talk with total strangers with ease. They feel a sense of loyalty and community. It is a "devotion" one needn't be ashamed to speak about at the water cooler or in a taxi cab.

The shopping mall is also a ritual for many. It is a monument to "the pursuit of happiness," freedom of choice, disbelief in thrift, temples to the Myth of Progress and Conspicuous Consumption. And most rock concerts are liturgies of the Id, the Child freed from the corset of the uptight week: noise, bombs, flashing lights, trashed guitars, half-clad bodies sweating, and an animal sense of belonging to a wild tribe.

Sacred Rituals

The difference between secular and religious rituals is that a sacred liturgy goes not only beyond everyday but beyond time itself. The object of such rituals is the *Mysterium Tremendum*.

"Religion" comes from the word *ligare* which means "to bind together" and the prefix *"re-"* which means "over and over." Prayer is religion in action; the words are only a means of putting oneself in union with God, open and expectant, a *CONNECTION* with the power and energy of the "overwhelming mystery."

For primitive societies the root of magic was that *soul*—the *anima mundi*—permeates the universe, and it gives everything its purpose and meaning, and one can relate to it I to Thou. Thus the whole universe is a sacrament: a vehicle of holiness. Native American medicine men, Eskimo shamans, Druid priests were trying not to manipulate the gods but, as Wordsworth put it, "to see into the heart of things," to put themselves in accord with the gods' messages through nature and achieve the wisdom to accept and trust them. Today we are no less gullible in our belief that technology, the new magic, can control "the gods of nature"— provided it doesn't destroy nature first, as it did its gods.

Ironically, especially in sophisticated societies such as our own, rituals can often be an obstacle to religious experience, not only when they are poorly executed, but even when they are scrupulously carried out as if they were a "performance" or the coronation of a European monarch, forgetting that an ordinary table in an ordinary room was satisfactory for the first one.

Also formal religious rites can become a *substitute* for genuine religious experience, often because many would prefer it that way, rather than risk the uncertainties of contact with the Unknown. Rituals are not intended to produce belief. Rather, they intend to provoke a response to the numinous, but if they are going to work a change within the participants, they have to count on religious belief *beforehand.* In none of the four gospels does Jesus ever perform a miracle to elicit belief but only in *response* to it: "Your faith has saved you" (Luke 7:50).

Nor can one expect to walk into a church "cold," not having had any other contact with God during the week, and expect to get "zapped"—any more than one would expect to fall in love forever on the first date. It would be a rare Sunday when everyone in the congregation is "up" at the same time. What we bring to the sacraments—especially the eucharist—is not our momentary selves but our *true* selves. If both the priest and the people are "genuine," then it will "work."

Ritual is never individualistic or private. Rather, it is a public expression of one's beliefs, buoyed by all the others into realizing I am not alone. Yoga, for instance, is not strictly speaking "worship." It could be merely communication with the inner self or a retirement into psychic numbness. Ritual is effective only if there is that "connection"—not with the words—but with the transcendent God present in immanent reality. Religion *means* "connection."

The Incarnation

As we have seen, some views of God, like paganism and pantheism, make God too immanent, too locked within nature and therefore controllable. At the opposite extreme other views, like Platonism and Deism, make God too transcendent, too aloof and unreachable. Both are right, and both are wrong, because neither is corrected by the truths within the other. God is both the immanent God of Hosea who seeks out the wayward, and the transcendent God of Job who is not answerable to us.

The ancient heroes of Israel, like Moses, stood as a kind of focal point, a lightning rod, where the power of God intersected with the people. Like the priest, he or she passed the needs of the people on to God and mediated God's answers back to them. But in Jesus, the hero *is* God *and* the people, at once. Thus he is God offered to humankind and humankind offered to God.

> He always had the nature of God,
>   But he did not think that by force he
>   should try to remain equal with God.
> Instead of this, of his own free will
>   he gave up all he had,
>   and took the nature of a servant.
> He became like a human being
>   and appeared in human likeness.
> He was humble and walked the
>   path of obedience all the way
>   to death—
>   his death on the cross.
> For this reason God raised him
>   to the highest place above
> and gave him the name that is
>   greater than any other name. . . .
> And all will openly proclaim that
>   Jesus Christ[1] is Lord.
>   *(Philippians 2:6–9, 11)*

---

1. When speaking of the Son of God's historical presence on earth, during the time the gospels describe, theologians refer to him as *"Jesus."* When speaking of the risen Son of God, still human but glorified in heaven, they use the term *"Christ."*

This does not mean that the Son stopped being God when incarnated into the man Jesus: he was "of divine status," the Word—the Self-expression—of the Father, who did not treat the status of divine dignity a privilege to be clutched at. Instead, he "emptied himself." He did not empty himself of divinity but of the privileges of it, including the divine knowledge, to become just like us, finding his way step by step without any exceptional privileges. He did that out of obedience to the Father, even to the humiliation of death on a cross. As a result God "superexalted" him and gave him "the name which is above all others": *Kyrios,* "Lord," a word Jews used as a substitute for the unspeakable name, "YHWH."

Jesus was not a "symbol" of God; he was the Real Thing, and in the eucharist, the bread and wine are not just "symbols" of God, they are the Real Thing.

The controversies in the early Church about the God-Man nature of Jesus, oddly enough, are mirrored in today's Biblical movies. One set of heresies held Jesus was only human—but raised to near-divine status, a human being but not fully divine; that view is reflected in *Jesus Christ, Superstar* and *The Last Temptation of Christ.* At the other extreme, a set of heresies held that Jesus was always God and only "appeared like" a human being. That view is reflected even in very fine films like *Jesus of Nazareth.* Jesus looks almost totally unworldly, somehow distressed at having to be with these "worldly" people. Both extremes base themselves on the antagonism we saw from the outset: the radical difference between the sacred and the secular, spirit and matter, transcendent and immanent. They cannot cope with the fact that Jesus was *both,* the unspeakably holy Son of God and yet also a secular man accused of eating and drinking with a relish unbecoming a holy man. Filmmakers ought to look

at Mother Teresa's face: an almost otherworldly serenity coupled
with the unstoppable determination of a runaway train.

A sacrament is a visible symbol of an inward grace, and Jesus
is grace made visible. As Edward Schillebeeckx, O.P., puts it,
Jesus *is* the sacrament of God, God not only present but visible,
filled with grace and ready to enliven souls with the superalive-
ness of God. In him, the transcendent *fused* with the immanent.
Like the pole at the center of the primitive village, like the cross,
like the cathedral, the God-Man Jesus is rooted in the earth and
reaching to the heavens. "I am the real vine" (John 15:1). As sap
rises out of the roots through the vine into the branches, so the
aliveness of the Father—grace—rises into Jesus and into us. In
the eucharist we offer God ordinary gifts, bits of bread and a cup
of wine, and—relying on the word of Christ—we ask God to
infuse into our gifts—and thence into us—the living presence of
the God-Man Jesus Christ, just as the Son fused himself into the
man Jesus. The risen Jesus—the glorified Christ—is a *dialogue*
between God and the community, the channel through whom
the enlivening Spirit of God comes to us.

The Church as the Sacrament of Christ

Just as the Spirit of God was embodied in Jesus, now after Jesus'
exaltation as the Christ, that same Spirit is embodied in the
Church. As Jesus was the sacrament of God, the Church is the
sacrament of Jesus. Jesus Christ was the first Church and, as
Augustine said, Christ died *so that* this new Church could be
born. When we enter the Church, we enter Christ. This does not
mean only the "official" Church, which we mean when we say
things like "When is the Church going to . . . ?" It means *all*

of us: pope and peasant, baroness and bag lady, king and cab driver. We now are the Body of Christ, who has no hands but ours, no voice but ours, no heart but ours.

The Church's first theologian, Paul, describes it:

> Christ is like a single body, which has many parts; it is still one body, even though it is made up of different parts. In the same way, all of us, whether Jews or Gentiles, whether slaves or free, have been baptized into the one body by the same Spirit, and we have all been given the one Spirit to drink. . . . So then, the eye cannot say to the hand, "I don't need you!" Nor can the head say to the feet, "Well, I don't need you!" On the contrary, we cannot do without the parts of the body that seem to be weaker, and those parts that we think aren't worth very much are the ones which we treat with greater care. . . . And so there is no division in the body, but all its different parts have the same concern for one another. If one part of the body suffers, all the others parts suffer with it; if one part is praised, all the other parts share its happiness. All of you are Christ's body.
>
> *(1 Corinthians 12:12–13, 21–23, 25–27)*

Just as the whole planet is a body with a soul, the *anima mundi,* so the Church is a body with a soul, the Holy Spirit. We are all interrelated parts. If the individual body has a toothache, it affects all the rest; if some people violate the ecology of the planet for their own profit, all of us—as Chief Seattle said—are violated; if part of the Church is suffering, we all suffer, at least in our compassion. Conversely, just as the leg or elbow has life only when it's connected to the body and its heart, so the Christian life is possible only in connection to the Body of Christ. It is not "my" grace, but a grace I share with the entire Body, the Church.

Each of us has a place in the workings of the Church; we are all ministers, not merely sheep waiting to be ministered to: "I come not to be served but to serve" (Mark 10:45). There are places you go where no priest would be welcome, people you meet who haven't been in a church in years. Not all of us can govern within the Church, preach great homilies, administer the sacraments, but we can all serve. St. Paul says in the same epistle:

> There are different kinds of spiritual gifts, but the same Spirit gives them. There are different ways of serving, but the same Lord is served. There are different abilities to perform service, but the same God gives ability to all for their particular service. The Spirit's presence is shown in some way in each person for the good of all.
>
> *(1 Corinthians 12:4–7)*

The point, obviously, is service—not the "importance" or even the "effectiveness," just serving. Priests' service is administering the sacraments and the care of souls, but the care of souls is not *solely* for priests. The root of the word "minister" is *ministrare*, not to rule, but "to serve." Parents care for the souls of their children, but also for those of their neighbors and fellow-workers: which ones are not living life as abundantly as they could? Students serve by studying in order to be of greater service later on, not merely wage-earners but healers. But life for students doesn't begin when they "get out into the real world."

Where are they now? Everywhere they look there are souls; which ones are not living life as abundantly as they could? Business people must serve, not merely negatively by their lack of dishonesty, but positively in their solicitousness for those who will be affected by their decisions; which ones are not living life as abundantly as they could? Managers must have concern for their workers; which ones are not living as abundantly as they could?

We often undersell our worth, focusing too ardently on our shortcomings, forgetting we serve a God who had no problem creating a universe out of nothing, and a Brother who could work miracles with materials as unpromising as mud and spittle.

The Greek word for "Church" is *ek-klesia*, "called forth." We are thus not just a group of Jesus' admirers. We are engrafted into the One Who Was for Others.

The human Jesus was the perfect respondent to God's call; he showed us a divine way to be human, a human way of being God. In Christ, divinity and humanity fuse, interpenetrating one another. Thus, the saving acts of the man, Jesus, were and are performed by a *divine* person. Therefore those actions were and are sacramental, because a sacrament is a bestowal of divine aliveness in an outwardly visible form. Because the human acts of Jesus were the acts of a *timeless* God, those acts are not restricted to the time-limited historical Jesus. They go on, now. "Jesus Christ is the same yesterday, today, and forever" (Hebrews 13:8).

As Schillebeeckx writes: "Because this [sacrament] is a personal act of God the Son—even though done in human form—it transcends time and space, and therefore in the literal sense of the word, like the soul in the body, becomes incarnate in time."

Thus, the actions of the risen Christ in the Church today are as effectual as the actions of Jesus. The sacraments are Christ, working visibly among his people, and we too are "called forth"

---

to be sacraments wherever we go, channels of grace for others to more abundant life.

Sacraments

Carl Jung said that most of the mental patients he had treated in a lifetime as a psychiatrist had lost their faith and therefore had no religion or church to help them live a symbolic life. "There had not been one whose problem in the last resort was not that of finding a religious outlook on life." The Catholic myth—its symbol system—is embodied principally in seven rituals called sacraments.

The original meaning of *sacramentum* was a pledge of good faith that bonded two people together. Therefore, a sacrament is a pledge on God's part, through Jesus Christ, to honor a commitment to Christ's Body, the Church, just as God had made a commitment to Israel in the Covenant to "be with" them.

As we have seen, the whole world is a "sacrament," the physical vehicle through which we apprehend the *anima mundi;* Jesus was the sacrament of God, the physical presence of the Holy Spirit; and since the exaltation of Jesus, the Church is the physical Body through which God honors Jesus' promises of grace: the super-aliveness of the Trinity. If the analogy is not too clumsy: the Energy is the Spirit of Christ, the Church is the storage place, and the sacraments are seven special outlets.

Grace is by no means restricted to the sacraments. As we have seen, a mother consoling a child in trouble, boys shaving their heads for their friend, a father welcoming home his wayward boy can be channels of grace: love undeserved. But some visible forms of invisible grace have become in the tradition of the

Church more important than others. The sacraments are different from other symbols because what they connect us to is not just "a value" but the *Mysterium Tremendum;* they are encounters with the glorified Christ. They celebrate *changes,* rites of passage, in one's relationship with God through the Body of Christ. The love of God for us is there, even for those who have run away, even for those who have never felt at home in the Church. The sacraments don't bring into existence something that was never there. Rather, they celebrate our new *awareness* that God's love and aliveness are there, for us.

It is important to understand that the sacraments are not *things,* like "eye of newt" or New Age crystals. They are encounters, through the physical symbols, with the risen Lord who was and is *the* sacrament. The seven sacraments are *actions,* not things, actions the assembled Church ("Whenever two or three are gathered in my name. . . .") performs and is enriched by, not things we "receive" or things "done to us." As Tad Guzie writes, "The Church is a *we* not an *it,"* though, by the middle ages, the Church—most of us—had come to be considered merely "recipients."

The sacraments are not magic—manipulating the gods of nature with incantations, and yet they *are!* Our sins are *gone,* forgotten as if they had never happened! At the eucharist, God has entered our bellies as the Spirit quickened Jesus in Mary's womb! In marriage and Holy Orders, our lives are utterly changed! In confirmation our lives can never be the same again! In baptism, a child has received a call, and her parents have accepted it until she is able to ratify it herself. In that near-final anointing, we *know* death will not have the final victory! It's *magic,* at least in the sense that the human eye is magic, that the mystery of love is magic, that the stirring in my heart at a summer sky ablaze with stars is *magic!* Enchantment, aliveness, an end to the Didi-Gogo rat race! Mr. Godot is here!

The sacraments don't work the way peyote works for a Navajo or the way a temple prostitute worked for a Baal worshipper. They are not "automatic." No sacrament can change anyone unless he or she has a genuine feeling of a *need* to be changed. Reconciliation is not a car wash; eucharist is not a vitamin pill, anointing is not a painkiller. Like the forgiveness of the father of the prodigal, no sacrament can work unless we want it to work.

The Reformation taught us lessons, many of which we did not "hear" until 400 years later. Its leaders called attention, rightly, to the role of *personal* faith and involvement in order for sacraments to be effective—contrary to the official Church's defense of *ex opere operato* (the sacrament effects a change no matter what, which we shall see more fully later). But they took all the "magic" out of the Christian life. Granted, there had been too much magic—indulgences, relics, atonement after one had already been forgiven. But the Reformers went too far. They "disenchanted" the presence of God in our symbolic lives. Some say that the liturgical changes since Vatican II, though very much needed, did the same thing in stressing historical correctness in the prayers and rituals of the Mass rather than a concern for meaningful symbols to satisfy the soul-needs of the faithful.

But if one's receptivity—one's "attitude"—can block the flow of grace in a sacrament, what about the case of a child receiving baptism before he or she can make any kind of personal response or the "last rites" for someone in a coma and equally incapable of any personal response? In neither case is there an ability actively to accept the grace. In such cases, the sacrament is not for the child or for the person hovering at the edge of death: it is for *us,* the assembled cell of the Church, so that we can be buoyed in hope, reminded of the infinite (not finite) background against which we measure importance.

When a priest, deacon, or layperson baptizes, it is, as St. Augustine said, "really Christ himself who baptizes." The *Constitution on the Liturgy* (7) says, "It is Christ himself who speaks when the scriptures are read in the church." When the sick person is anointed, it is Christ himself who is present. "Where two or three come together in my name, I am there with them" (Matthew 18:20). And this is the Jesus Christ who could work miracles with mud and spittle. Leave it to the theologians to figure out "how." And they are at odds with themselves and will be till the final trumpet.

But the Church declares that a sacrament works *ex opere operato,* that is, "merely by the fact that the operation has been performed." No matter how sinful the minister, if the recipient (or the persons present) is open to the grace, the sacrament effects a real change within them. This is not a personal power in the priest; he is merely an agent, just as this word processor is not writing this page but is merely a means. Even Jesus said, "The words that I have spoken to you do not come from me. The Father, who remains in me, does his own work" (John 14:10). So, too, the minister. Contrary to the accusations of the Reformers, the Church does not hold that sacraments are magic, in the strict sense: laying on obligation on God. They do not depend on the "purity" of the minister or the formulas said without a single misspeaking. Nor does the faith of the recipient "oblige" God. The sacrament is *Christ's* act: an act of grace, an act of love undeserved. Christ has freely chosen to give grace—an intensity of inner aliveness—when the recipient genuinely wants it, just as the father of the prodigal gave forgiveness when his son asked for it, just as Jesus gave healing in response to faith.

Each sacrament is, as the book's title suggests, *a rite of passage,* a privileged moment, but only one moment in a *process.*

The focal, core sacrament is the eucharist, at the heart of the Church's life, the central act of gratitude, the body and blood of Christ enlivening the Body of Christ. Branching from that central "heart" are sacraments of *initiation* (baptism and confirmation), *healing* (reconciliation and anointing the sick), and *ministry* (order and matrimony)—all of which have their roots in the heart: eucharist. But one could also make a case that baptism and confirmation are also sacraments of ministry, since at those moments we are "ordained" Christians, which is synonymous with service.

In every sacrament, we tend to focus only on the isolated *act* when the sacrament is publicly solemnized. But a marriage, for instance, isn't restricted to the time of the wedding. It is a process of *becoming* married, which began long before the rite and will continue to grow; couples in their fifties are far *more* married than they were on their wedding day.

Any sacrament is a rite of passage in an ongoing *relationship.* Baptism is only the beginning of membership in this Family, and it is the task of the parents and godparents to see that it never ceases to intensify. Confirmation is a personal commitment to a relationship with God through the Body of Christ, to be more than a mere passive member but to become a minister of the more abundant life. Reconciliation heals that relationship, encountering the forgiveness of Christ, and a reminder that we too often sell short our dignity as daughters and sons of God. Anointing heals the soul who feels abandoned by God, putting this suffering *into* the Body of Christ on Calvary, which paradoxically was the doorway to rebirth. Holy orders quite obviously is a radical change in an individual's relationship with the Body of Christ. The eucharist is a coming-home each week, to be reminded of who we are and what we are for, to re-charge the Spirit in us. Each of the sacraments is not merely a once-for-all rite but a high point in a lifelong *process*.

The more we are estranged from nature, the less meaningful sacraments become. Water is trivial, something you wash in, swim in, hidden away in pipes. We have lost the taste of bread unless it's slathered with peanut butter. Wine is nothing unless you've had too much. Oil is for salads and suntans. Thus in our Gradgrind world, the sacraments become for many a morgue of symbols.

The purpose of the rest of this book is to attempt to revivify those symbols. Which, whether successful or not, is a very Christian enterprise. The whole message of Christianity is about resurrection and rebirth: more abundant life!

Chapter Six

THE CENTRAL SACRAMENT: EUCHARIST

Think of it, Wat! God, in a bit of bread, come to bring morning into the darkness of our bellies! Hosannah!"

—H. F. M. Prescott,
A Man on a Donkey

A Puzzlement

On the night he was betrayed, Jesus took bread, gave thanks, and gave it to his friends, saying, "Take this, all of you, and eat it. This *is* my body, which will be given up for you." Then he took the cup, gave thanks, and gave it to his friends: "This *is* the cup of my blood, the blood of the new and everlasting covenant. It will be shed for you, and for all, so that sins may be forgiven. Do this in memory of me" (from Matthew 26:26–28).

But what does it mean?

Deaths and Rebirths

The very first question to face about the eucharist is the very bold one: "Why bother?"—especially when whatever idealistic books say about the eucharist is embedded concretely in a ceremony which is, quite frankly, too often deadly dull. It's a very legitimate question, and one wishes more Catholics had the courage to pose it to their pastors if they believe the liturgy they are "forced" to attend is totally irrelevant to their lives.

"Why should I go if I get nothing out of it? Why can't I just pray out in the woods?" Both very reasonable questions. The first question in response, however, might be: "When was the last time you actually *did* go out and pray in the woods?" Often that objection is raised by people more interested in winning an argument or getting out of an obligation than in finding the truth. Second, praying out in the woods during the week is a terrific idea, and if you did it, the Mass would be less boring— guaranteed. Third, the meaningfulness of the Mass is in direct proportion to your personal *commitment* to the life in Christ. For the half-hearted, the Mass will surely be half-hearted, just as with any relationship—a friendship, a job, a marriage—gives back only what you put into it. If you "allow" God to exist only when you have a sick child or a test for which you haven't studied or a job in jeopardy, the Mass will be no more than a dreary soup kitchen where you occasionally go for a handout.

The pivotal question about the eucharist is whether—in the one go-round you have with life—you're missing out on something others have, something very important, without it.

If you have the time and inclination to stand back and look at your life, you realize that it is all—over and over—a series of invitations to "deaths" and better "re-births."

In his book, *Cosmos,* Carl Sagan, no minor prophet among modern reductionists, says that the marvelous species which arose in evolution and then died out—dinosaurs, trilobites, pterodactyls—does not argue to a very efficient creator. Of course. Because efficiency isn't as high on the creator's list of priorities as it is on Carl Sagan's. Perhaps more than any modern scientist, God seems to delight in experiments. Then moving on.

That tendency in God is evident not only in the millions of years of evolution but in every single human life, the cycles of which are, as we saw, the same now as 30,000 years ago. Birth itself is, paradoxically, a "little death." For nine months, we floated serenely in the womb, warm, fed, without a worry in the world. Then suddenly, through no fault of our own, we are forcibly ejected out into the cold and noise, and by that very fact of being born, we are ultimately condemned eventually to die. Weaning and potty-training are "little deaths," losing that carefree life where everything was done for us, but without that loss we would never possess any independence. In the play years Mommy boots us out into the cold to play with the other children, but without that loss we would never learn to solve our own disputes without an adult around. Kindergarten is a sometimes heartbreaking loss, stranded among strangers by a Mommy we had always thought was the Fairy Godmother, but without that "little death" we would never begin to learn the skills to cope with life on our own. In adolescence, the child "dies" so that the adult can emerge like a butterfly from a cocoon. Marriage is a death to self, to "unlimited" freedom, but a sacrifice one is willing to make for the joy of never again being alone. Parenthood is just such a sacrifice: "death" and "rebirth" as a person far richer than before. A couple could live their lives serenely together, but instead they commit themselves to other lives, to 20-plus years of apprehension, unpayable bills, broken arms, outgrown clothes, mediocre grades—but also the joy, the pride, the sense of having contributed life to life. Old age comes as a "little death," too, but it is the opportunity to savor, to sit back and see life as a coherent story, to find wisdom. Death and rebirth, you see, are the law of human life. Conversion.

The entire Old Testament is also testimony that the will of God is death and rebirth, over and over. When the experiment in the Garden of Eden had failed, Yahweh gave them a second chance. In the story of the Flood, Yahweh had Noah and his family start over. Yahweh called Abraham and Sarah from Ur of the Chaldees to head south and start yet again. When the Hebrews were languishing in slavery in Egypt, Yahweh sent Moses to challenge the Pharaoh and lead the people through the desert to Canaan to begin again. When the people had been led off again in slavery to Babylon, Yahweh finally led them back to Jerusalem to start over.

In the Incarnation, God went through those same stages of "death" and "rebirth" which every human being has undergone since the Cro-Magnons. In fact, his first "death" was the Incarnation itself, surrendering the privileges of the divinity in order to learn as we do, step by step, with no assurances. Although Jesus never shared the agonies and joys of parenthood, he did have twelve rather taxing "sons." And he surely knew the death which awaits us all. But Augustine says he believed Jesus went to his death as eagerly as a bridegroom goes to his bride, because he trusted what lay beyond. In the twelfth century, Peter Abelard wrote that Jesus did not die as a ransom for sinful humanity or as a penalty to "buy off" a vengeful God. Rather, the atonement achieved by Jesus was an atonement, a fusion of all humankind with God. For centuries humanity had been yearning for God and God had been yearning for humanity. At last the two intersected in Jesus on the cross. Convergence and conversion. That is what eucharist celebrates.

The gospel is not about death; it is about life, rebirth. "I've come that you may have life, and have it more abundantly." But the only way to *new* life is through surrender of the *old* life. Conversion is not just a coat you put on to go to church. It means to *lose* the old self, as Jesus did both at the Incarnation and at the crucifixion. "Unless a grain of wheat fall into the ground and die. . . ."

"We write to you about the Word of life, which has existed from the very beginning. We have heard it, and we have seen it with our eyes; yes, we have seen it, and our hands have touched it. . . . What we have seen and heard we announce to you also, so that you will join with us in the fellowship that we have with the Father and with his Son Jesus Christ. We write this in order that our joy may be complete" (1 John 1:1, 3–4).

Like all the changes life inflicts on us, that is one more invitation we can refuse, the invitation to more abundant life.

124   WILLIAM J. O'MALLEY

Meals

There is a real difference between ingesting food and sharing a meal. When they're hungry, little kids are very much interested in food, but they're not much interested in sharing a meal. Conversation makes the difference, and the conversation part makes them fidget and want to "be excused." But for adults somehow the conversation and the food improve one another. Even young people know that peanut-butter-and-jelly becomes less boring when they eat with their friends in the cafeteria. There is probably nothing lonelier than going to a nice restaurant, ordering an out-of-the-ordinary meal, and eating alone, with families and friends all over the room laughing and talking. And we don't ordinarily consider dining with complete strangers, say at a formal banquet, a meal. Rather it's a chore. Perhaps that is why the liturgy is so often a chore: we don't know—or care about—the other people in the room, as we do when a Mass is celebrated in the home or with a homeroom in school.

The conversation at the Last Supper wasn't much different from an ordinary Sunday Mass today. In the longest description (John 13–17), the conversation is more nearly a monologue, in which with a few interventions from the disciples Jesus speaks of: (1) his "going to the Father" and its necessity for their sake; (2) the relationship Jesus and his followers must have with "the world"; (3) the role of the Holy Spirit in their future; (4) the glorification that awaits him; (5) the commandment to love. All of which, despite three years of intensive training, the disciples found completely befuddling, as their few interventions prove. They were just like ourselves, their innermost selves and values concentrated on getting ahead.

For Jesus, his approaching death is central to the Last Supper, and yet the disciples seem to have no sense of his—and their—imminent doom. Later, even after they had gone through the trauma of the crucifixion, and the overwhelming experience of Jesus reborn from death, and perhaps a month more when the risen Jesus stayed with them, their very last question to Jesus before his ascension was: "Lord, will you at this time give the Kingdom back to Israel?" (Acts 1:6). They were still hankering to sit on those thrones, to find who would be "first in the Kingdom." It wasn't until the Spirit came upon them at Pentecost that they finally understood, and that understanding not only made the celebration of the Lord's Supper a memorial alive with meaning but it made their martyrs' deaths alive with meaning, too.

Until you can *feel* within yourself that experience of the reality of death and the reality of rebirth, you will never *feel* the reality of the Lord's Supper—even when it is well done.

Passover

At the Passover celebration, Israel recalls the days of its enslavement, which they can never forget—just as they can never now forget the Holocaust. They have done it year after year since hundreds of years before Christ. As they set the Passover table with unleavened bread, a shank of lamb, wine, bitter herbs, an egg, they put themselves into a multidimensional meditation on who they are as a people. It is the Passover because the vengeance of Yahweh passed over their ancestors' blood-spattered doorposts while the Egyptian firstborn were slain. It is the Feast of Unleavened Bread, "the bread of affliction." But most important of all, it is "the day of our freedom."

Before the celebration begins, the entire family hunts through the house to be sure no leavened bread or cake or beer is there. If they are to set out free and fresh, they must have no contamination from the past. Like their ancestors, they will begin the year over again with the "bread made in haste," without waiting for it to rise. For every year's Jews, "the day of our freedom" is not just the once-for-all freedom of those ancestral slaves from Egypt, but the freedom of all those around this table at this time: a commitment to start the year fresh, clean, free. This is a memorial of a "then" which becomes a "now."

Each new generation must "enter into" the bitter experience of slavery, try to relive it as if they themselves had endured it, let it seep into their very bones: being held in contempt, the deep alienation and rejection, feeling there is no escape from the vicious circles of violence. Without that deep sense of enslavement, they have no way to appreciate what the liberation of Exodus meant—and means. Just as resurrection means nothing to a Christian until he or she has a *felt* realization of death, so to a Christian or Jew, freedom means nothing without a *felt* realization of slavery.

Each year the Jews reexperience not only the cruelty of enslavement but the paralyzing effect of the *slave mentality,* the bleak conviction that nobody can do anything about anything, the helpless belief that everything is "out of our hands." The only thing we have in common is our inescapable powerlessness.

But in reenacting the Passover *seder,* Jews for the last 2,500 years have found hope (because the Lord has set them free before, again and again) and the courage to start fresh.

The Last Supper

Jesus celebrated Passover many times in his life, but his final seder was crucial to him, even though, given the time, it was not strictly speaking a Passover meal. Jesus, in fact, was killed on the Friday afternoon before Passover—just at the time the Passover lambs were being slaughtered.

Jesus took the unleavened bread out of which the new life of freedom comes, prayed, and then said, " 'This is my Body, which will be given up [broken] for you.' Then he took the final cup, prayed, and said, 'This is a cup of my blood, the blood of the new and everlasting covenant. It will be shed for you, and for all, so that sins may be forgiven. Do this in memory of me' "(from eucharistic Prayer II).

Just as Jesus' physical body made him present to them at that moment, so will this bread and wine be the extension of his physical self for the rest of time. But it is not just Jesus' presence the eucharist embodies but a *relationship:* his Body is "given up *for you*" and his Blood "shed *for you*" for the purpose of setting you free from your sins, from the anchors that keep you from growing. Jesus concluded by asking them to use this ceremony as a memorial of him, but a case could be made that he also was asking us that "sins may be forgiven" in his memory as well. ("As we forgive those who trespass against us.")

Like the Jews of Egypt—and all time since—we, too, are "a pilgrim people on earth." Our lives are a journey, and the eucharist is our compass and our manna.

As Dr. Monika Hellwig writes:

> Each time we celebrate we try to reach out to [Christ] as he reaches out to us. We try to enter

into the experience of his death and its meaning
to him and to us, trying to broaden our vision to
the dimensions of his vision, to raise our goals in
life to the height of his goals, and to overcome
the alienation and unfreedom and confusion of
our lives by bringing them into confrontation
with the utter freedom and simplicity of his
engagement with the Father.

As with the Passover *seder,* each Mass is a memorial of a
"then" which becomes a "now."

The Early Christian Mass

In the earliest churches, long before the conversion of
Constantine removed the danger of being Christian, Sunday was
the Lord's Day for them, but it was also a working day, so they
had to get up before dawn and make their way through the
streets to the home of a Christian family who had a large house.
Each family carried a small biscuit, hidden in their clothes,
because their religion was outlawed, and to be caught with it
could mean their lives. They slipped in by a back door where a
deacon looked them over to see if they were known and trusted;
spies were commonplace.

They moved on to a large living room where people milled
about, talking, Many of them they knew, since they met one or
two evenings during the week to pray together, hear instructions,
reflect on the letters of the apostles. There were no soldiers
present, even in civilian clothes; Christians were rigid pacifists,
and a soldier's oath entailed offering incense to the emperor. At
one end of the room sat an older man, the bishop of the city,

dressed like every other man in working clothes. Seated around him were several other men and women, the "elders" or "deacons" or "presbyters" (priests), very much like a parish council. The bishop stood and greeted the assembly, and all replied. Then they turned and embraced one another, moving freely about because there were no pews. It was a genuine sense of fellowship; they were all risking death to be there.

On a table in front of the bishop there was a small table, and on either side stood a deacon or deaconess, one holding a plate and the other a cup. Someone from every family filed up and put the biscuit they had brought onto the plate and poured a bit of wine into the cup. Then the bishop and elders stood with their hands outstretched over plate and cup, silently, focusing attention on the bread and wine which symbolized their unity as the Body of Christ. Then the bishop invited them to lift up their hearts as their offering and give thanks to the Lord, and chanted a short prayer to thank God for creation, for caring for them, and for their recreation as a new people in Christ.

Then the bishop broke a piece from a biscuit and ate it, then took three sips of wine while the deacon(esses) broke the rest. One by one the people filed up to the bishop, who said, "The bread of heaven in Christ Jesus," and each answered, "Amen," taking a piece of bread, then going to the cup. The cupholder said, "In God the Father almighty," and the person responded, "Amen," and took a first sip. As the person took the second and third sips, the cupholder said, "In the Lord Jesus Christ" and "In the Holy Spirit in the holy church."

There was no rush. This, after all, was the whole purpose in their coming together. At the end, the bishop gave a blessing, and some came forward for fragments of the bread to carry home for those who had been unable to be present because of illness or work.

There are elements there which might make our own liturgies more meaningful, especially the custom of milling about beforehand and renewing or making acquaintances and offering the sign of peace at the beginning of the service. There are many, however, old and young, who find that whole element of the Mass distasteful. That distaste is worth reflection. It is very real and at times strongly felt. But what does it say about the person who experiences it, about the very heart of what the Mass means? Does the gospel give us the option of being shy or, worse, anonymous? That repulsion at greeting strangers sounds very little like Jesus or his gospel. Perhaps a key there.

Eucharist

"Eucharist" comes from the Greek *eucharistia,* "giving thanks." It is motivated by the same beliefs that underlay the American feast of Thanksgiving: a realization that the harvest was not entirely their doing, gratitude for the good that had come out of their sufferings. (Though Gradgrind has co-opted the feast and made it the Feast When Xmas Selling Begins.)

But as we have seen, without a felt realization of death, the people and things we do honestly love gradually become taken for granted, as if we would always have them and—more importantly—as if we had done something to *deserve* them. Before I existed, how could I have done something to deserve existence? My parents could probably have had a far easier life if they had chosen to remain childless. Instead, without any guarantee at all how this "product" would turn out, they took the risk. Granted that if I had never existed, I wouldn't have known the difference. But I *do* exist and . . . *wow!* It would take me a month to write down the names of the people I love, the books that stir my heart, the moments that have taken my breath away, the scrapes I never thought I could survive. It's . . . wonder-filled!

But without a regular time to reflect on life, we tend to forget how *gifted* we have been. And gratitude—giving thanks, eucharist—depends on remembering.

The Church itself becomes a sacrament in the eucharist in that the liturgy brings the Church into being as the Body of Christ. But eucharist can "happen" only as an act of the Church *as* the Body of Christ. Vatican II completely reversed the idea that began in the Middle Ages which almost completely "priesti-fied" the eucharist, making the priest the only active agent in the Mass. Now we see that it is *Christ* who offers the liturgy through the priest *and* the body which is the Church. That change is clearest in what the priest used to say in preparation of the gifts and what the priest says now. Before, he said, "Accept . . . this spotless host which I, your unworthy servant, offer you"; now, he says, "Blessed are you, Lord God. Through your goodness *we* have these gifts to offer."

Vatican II gives the meaning of this act of the Church:

> At the Last Supper, on the night when he was betrayed, our Savior instituted the eucharistic sacrifice of his body and blood. He did this in order to perpetuate the sacrifice of the Cross through the centuries until he should come again, and so to entrust to his beloved spouse, the Church, a memorial of his death and resurrec-tion: a sacrament of love, a sign of unity, a bond of charity, a paschal banquet in which Christ is

eaten, the mind is filled with grace, and a pledge
of future glory is given to us."
(Constitution on the Sacred Liturgy, 47)

St. Paul draws his understanding from the Old Testament:
remembrance of the Passover and the liberation of the Exodus,
but now Jesus is our paschal lamb. John underlines that truth in
his gospel when he shows Jesus die at the same time the Passover
lambs were slain (John 19:31). The Mass, then, is not about
death—much less about sin; it is about the rebirth that can come
about through death.

There are four key concepts in the heart of the eucharist
emphasized by Vatican II: (1) it is a sacrament; (2) it is a remembrance; (3) it is an act of worship; (4) it is a communion or
fellowship.

Sacrament

Eucharist is no longer seen as a "holy thing" which is "given" by
the priest and "received" by the people. It is a sacred *action,* done
by a sanctified people gathered as the embodiment of Christ.

Remembrance

The liturgy of the word reminds us of our story: our roots in
Judaism and in the life of Christ and the early Church. In the
liturgy of the eucharist the wine reminds us that the blood
sprinkled on the Hebrews at Mt. Sinai was a sign of their
covenant; the wine consumed at Mass is "a cup of my blood, the

blood of the new and everlasting covenant." But the eucharist does not merely remind us of a single event: the Last Supper or the crucifixion. Rather as Passover reminds Jews not only of the night they awaited liberation but also of their trek through the desert and the blood covenant at Sinai, the eucharist reminds us of Holy Thursday, Good Friday, Easter Sunday, and the infusion of the Spirit into the Body of Christ on Pentecost—as a single liberating event.

Worship

Eucharist is an act of reverence and honor in gratitude to God, showing us clearly who God is and who we are, judged as Job was against the background of the *Mysterium Tremendum.* It is, as we saw, both an act of humility and an act of exaltation. In contrast to God, we are shadows in the Light; but because of the death, resurrection, and exaltation of the God-Man, Jesus Christ, we too have been "lifted up." Because of Christ, each of us is Cinderella.

Communion

All religion is a "connection," a transcendent reaching into the reality of God and an immanent reaching outward to our sisters and brothers. We unite ourselves to the story that gives our lives meaning (the liturgy of the word); we offer our innermost selves with the ordinary bits of bread and cup of wine ("We lift up our hearts"); we share ourselves outward to those around us (the greeting of peace) and then commune with God himself (the communion) in which the risen Christ who has fused himself into the bread and wine infuses that self-presence into us.

The eucharist—our thanksgiving—is to celebrate the reconciliation of God and humankind and of human beings with one another—and within ourselves. "Because there is the one loaf of bread, all of us, though many, are one body, for we all share the same loaf" (1 Corinthians 10:17). At least temporarily a bonding takes place, nurtured by the Host, who in this case is also the servant and the food. It is a communion among people not only divided from one another but conflicted even within themselves. It extends reconciliation to sisters and brothers: "Do this in memory of me." Doris Donnelly puts it:

> "The eucharist points to the possibility of bonding in the middle of rubble; it promises presence and power in the middle of devastation and feebleness; and in the middle of this century's persistent hunger for meaning, it offers signs of connectedness that link people to other people and to all the living things in the universe."

Our weekly giving-thanks is to make contact with people where they are, to enable them to see better, hear better, make more visible the reality of their faith and trust in Christ.

The Presence of Christ

Probably no doctrine—other than the question how Jesus could be both God and man—has divided dedicated Christians more than *how* Jesus manages to be present in the eucharist.

The two sides argued whether the bread and wine were "only" symbols (that is, merely "suggested" the presence of Christ) or really were the body and blood of Christ (as really, physically present as Jesus was at the Last Supper). But that puts the *things* involved in the eucharist (the bread and wine) as more important than the *relationship* between Christ and us. As Tad Guzie says, the objects in the eucharist are the "realizers of reality." When symbols become only reminders—signs, like product logos—they are no longer truly symbols. Take an analogy between the bread and wine on the one hand, and a wedding ring on the other. Does the wedding ring *embody* a real relationship between a man and a woman, or is it just one piece of jewelry among many when the relationship has died? If a woman or man lost it, would the prime question be the expense of replacing it? By the same token, in the eyes of the believers present, is the bread just the same "stuff" we put in the toaster? Is the wine just the same "stuff" we drink at high-class parties? Or do the symbols "carry" a far greater value?

Whether the words written in the gospel versions were the actual words of Jesus or whether they were formulas the early Christian communities used at their own recreation of the Last Supper and "read back into" the versions, it was clearly the faith-choice of early communities to use the words, "This *is* my Body . . . this *is* the cup of my blood." They did not say, "Let this be a reminder." Their faith chose the word "is."

Again, the emphasis was not on the *objects* on the communion table but on the *relationship* those objects focused: the crucified-resurrected-exalted Jesus Christ and the Body of believers his Spirit still energizes. The emphasis was on *breaking* the bread and *sharing* the cup. We too are to "break ourselves up" and "share" the pieces. Their interest was not in what happened to the bread and wine, but what happened to the *people*. John Chrysostom wrote, "Through the food the Lord has given us, we become members of his flesh and of his bones." We are "mixed into" that flesh, and "he has kneaded his body with ours." The purpose of Christianity is to transform *all* creation into Christ—the living presence of the transcendent among the immanent. The eucharist is a beginning: bits of creation are turned into Christ. And through the eucharist, the Word becomes flesh in *us*.

Will Rogers once said that, if preachers concentrated more on our savior's message and less on the means by which he arrived and departed this world, we'd all be a lot better off. Emperor Charles V tried the same ploy when he gathered representatives of Rome and each of the Protestant factions, begging them all to agree that at least *somehow* Jesus was *more* intensely present in the eucharist than anywhere else on earth. The God we believe in *somehow* created a universe out of nothing and *somehow* animated a human being with divinity. Such a God would surely have found no difficulty in fusing that same divinity into bread and wine. But, stubbornly, they refused, each nursing his own pet theory. How foolish. As foolish as trying to define strictly when and how love is present and when and how love is not.

For hundreds of years, the question of Christ's presence "at" the eucharist was focused almost exclusively on his presence "in" the eucharist: within the bread and wine. Vatican II broadened the scope of our understanding to center first on the eucharistic *action* and then, within that action, four distinct ways in which Christ is present: (1) in the assembled people, (2) in God's word, (3) in the priest, (4) and above all, in the bread and wine. Further, the council said, Christ is not present among us to be adored or ministered to; he is there *for us,* an active presence to be used as the channel between us and God and between God and us. There is only one Christ present in each eucharist, but he appears in different roles of the one action.

The risen Lord is present in the assembly ("Where two or more are gathered in my name, there am I in the midst of them"), and that presence unites them as his Body. The risen Lord is present in God's Word. As St. Augustine wrote, "It is Christ himself who speaks when holy scriptures are read." The risen Lord is present in the priest as the primary agent in action of the people's sacrament; to take a perhaps crude analogy, he is the lens through whom the power of the Spirit in the people focuses on the action. ("When anybody baptizes, it is really Christ who baptizes.") And the risen Lord is present in the food we share, to do and be what food has always done: nourish and unite. Each of the four ways of being present does what all symbols do: act as channels for grace.

The Protestant theologian, Karl Barth, articulates what a difference it makes to believe that the presence of the risen Lord actually is in not only the assembly and God's word and the priest but actually *in* the bread and wine:

> At those times when the task of being ministers of the divine word, as we of the Reformed Churches say, has oppressed us, have we not all felt a yearning for the rich services of Catholicism, and for the enviable role of the priest at the altar? When he elevates the *Sanctissimum* [the *Mysterium Tremendum*], with its full measure of that meaning and power which the *material* symbol enjoys over the symbol of the human word, the double grace of the sacrificial

death and the incarnation of the Son of God is not only preached in words but actually takes place in his hands.

The eucharist is a rite of passage whereby the eternal enters the everyday, the sacred energizes the secular, and empowers us to go on striving.

Chapter Seven

INITIATION: BAPTISM

In the beginning, when God created the universe, the earth was formless and desolate. The raging ocean that covered everything was engulfed in total darkness, and the Spirit of God was moving over the water.

(Genesis 1:1–2)

At that time Jesus arrived from Galilee and came to John at the Jordan to be baptized by him. But John tried to make him change his mind. "I ought to be baptized by you," John said, "and yet you have come to me!" But Jesus answered him, "Let it be so for now. For in this way we shall do all that God requires." So John agreed. As soon as Jesus was baptized, he came up out of the water. Then heaven was opened to him, and he saw the Spirit of God coming down like a dove and lighting on him. Then a voice said from heaven, "This is my own dear Son, with whom I am pleased."

(Matthew 3:13–17)

A Puzzlement

> For surely you know that when we were baptized
> into union with Christ Jesus, we were baptized
> into union with his death. By our baptism, then,
> we were buried with him and shared his death, in
> order that, just as Christ was raised from death
> by the glorious power of the Father, so also we
> might live a new life. . . . And we know that
> our old being has been put to death with Christ
> on his cross, in order that the power of the sinful
> self might be destroyed, so that we should no
> longer be the slaves of sin.
>
> *(Romans 6:3–4)*

What does that mean?

Initiation

Each of us has been initiated more than a few times. The first days of grade school, high school, college, the people who have been there longer go out of their way to ease the embarrassment and the disorientation, to make you feel at "home" and help you fit in—when you don't feel at home at all and feel you're sticking out like a skunk at a garden party. It is called "orientation," getting your bearings against a whole new background. When each of those levels of education is over, a ritual celebrates not only that you have graduated *out of* the past stage but also that it is a "commencement" *into* a new one. Some have been inducted into the military services, the National Honor Society, the

Scouts, a fraternity or sorority, and—with the sponsorship of a full member and after a period of probation—the group holds a ceremony to signify that you are no longer just one of "them" but are one of "us." The ceremony embodies a change in status, a conversion. This is what baptism is: an initiation, an orientation against a whole new background, a graduation from one way of looking at life and the commencement of a new one. It is the ritualization of a complete conversion.

In the very early Church, baptism, confirmation, and first communion were an integrated single rite, usually only for adults, which took place only once a year at the Vigil of Easter. It was a fitting, highly symbolic time, since St. Paul had said (see Puzzlement) the whole imagery of baptism recaptures Christ's death and rebirth, which is the core of Christianity. The community gathered with the bishop in a large home, singing, meditating on scripture, praying for the candidates who waited outside praying with their sponsors and deacons(esses). It was an all-night vigil.

Just before dawn, those who had completed a catechumenate which sometimes lasted three years of instructions, exorcisms, and testing, and who had fasted for the past two days, gathered outside around the pool with their sponsors who had attested to their good conduct, especially in works of charity. They removed all their clothing, symbolizing putting off their old lives. (Quite likely out of modesty men and women were baptized separately, therefore the need for deaconesses.) The deacon or deaconess invited them to foreswear paganism, then anointed them with ordinary olive oil, a symbol of the "everyday" they were leaving behind. Then they led them, naked as Adam and Eve, down the steps into the water. Above them, a priest asked the three baptismal questions: Do you believe in the Father, the Son, and the Holy Spirit? And the candidates responded to each, "I do believe," and at each response the deacon or deaconess submerged the candidate under the water, a ritual drowning into the body of Christ's death, from which each time they emerged again and breathed life.

The newly baptized came out of the water, dried themselves, and were anointed once again, but this time with the perfumed oil of thanksgiving (chrism) to symbolize their new life. They put on new white garments and, each holding a lighted candle, filed into "the Church," where the bishop laid his hands on each one in turn, praying they might be worthy receptacles of the Holy Spirit. Then he anointed each again with the perfumed oil of thanksgiving, signifying their acceptance into the People of God, (which later became the separate sacrament of confirmation), kissed them and welcomed them into the Body. Then the celebration concluded with the new Christians' first eucharist.

Meaning

That ritual at dawn on Easter Sunday morning was only the final, culminating moment in a long process of gradual but total *conversion,* a complete turnabout from a life of self-absorption to a life of self-giving. At first, the person might have been puzzled by the other-worldly serenity of a Christian neighbor amid all the brutality and selfishness all around them, or was puzzled by the neighbor's kindness to the most unpleasant people. Redemption means liberation, setting free. People around could see a change of attitude, a conversion, from apprehension to serenity. They lived differently from the way they had before and from the way most people lived: no longer harried, offering one another support, consolation, funds when they were in need. Even in times of persecution, personal failure, bereavement, they had a totally different perspective: the resurrection.

This of course is why the Church grew so quickly. ("Can I see your freedom? Can I feel your joy?") People saw what liberation from the chaos of life meant, not in theory but in the everyday lives of Christians, and they wanted to understand it, experience it, share it. So the inquisitive neighbors made inquiries and, after a period of scrutiny to be sure they were not spies, were introduced into a first understanding of the gospel message. Then, after long instruction, they were enrolled among those to be baptized at the Easter vigil.

After such a long process and such a vivid ceremony, newly baptized Christians had no doubt whatever that they were "completely new," beginning a totally different way of looking at life, dealing with their neighbors, their work, their families. And they knew they were completely "different" from their pagan neighbors because of that. Although most of us were baptized as infants when we were unaware of the symbolism, and although many of the symbols have been thinned by propriety (no nakedness, no total immersion, no complete change of clothing) and further thinned by our culture's detachment from natural symbols like water, fire, oil—being a genuine Christian should still make one feel dramatically "different." Gradually since the Enlightenment, the Industrial Revolution, the triumph of rationalism and utilitarianism, and with lightning acceleration in the last 50 years of the technological age, our culture has become as irreligious as pagan Rome. The contrast between a life of self-absorption and a life of self-giving is once again as dramatic is it was then. An interesting question then is: if being a real Christian were a punishable crime today, as it was then, could the authorities find enough solid evidence of it from studying our weekly actions even to bring charges against us?

Like each of the other sacraments, baptism is about achieving a newer, richer *freedom*—freedom from the constraints of others' expectations, from what "everybody says" will make us happy and fulfilled as human beings, even of our deadly awareness of our own shortcomings. Freedom in the Christian sense is that you have courage and self-confidence (or Christ-confidence) enough that we can put ourselves at the disposal of others. The hippest, most arrogant haven't that kind of courage and self-confidence. That sort of freedom seemed "folly" to the Greeks, who classical culture thought were the epitome of how human beings should live. No. To be genuinely Christian means that our self-absorption and self-protectiveness are "disabled," in order that we can be free to serve others.

Baptism *introduces* us to a community *through which* we *can* be outfitted to face the tasks of secular life in a more dignified way than others. But, as we have seen so often before, baptism is an invitation we can refuse, even though in infancy others accepted it for us. Being free, we may choose *not* to be free.

Water

In Greek, *bapto* means "to dye" a garment to change its color, and the more intensive form, *baptizo* means "to cause to perish," as in drowning. When speaking of more commonplace ritual cleansings, Greeks used less dramatic words like "wash, rinse, sprinkle." Thus, the early Church did not think of this action as an everyday ritual. It was life-changing.

Water is a very positive symbol. Our planet is the only one we know of which is blue. All human life came out of those blue waters; each one of us lived nine months in the water in our mother's womb, and our bodies are 70 percent water. Water quenches thirst; we can go a full month without much food, but only five days without water. We use water to cleanse our bodies, our homes, to water lawns, fill pools, extinguish fires. Without water and the sun, we could grow no food. Perhaps young city people have no felt understanding of the "sacredness" of an oasis to a desert nomad, but the toughest city kid knows the joy of opening a fire hydrant in July and frolicking in water.

Yet, like human nature, water has its dark side: floods destroy homes, crops, human lives; polluted water carries disease; storms can wipe out whole coastlines. Anyone used to swimming in calm lakes knows the terror of water when swimming in the ocean the first time and being caught and hurled head over heels in the breakers. Anyone caught at sea in a storm, as the apostles were, understands the panic water can raise. It was out of the chaos of the primeval waters that God brought cosmos, and the two forces have been in conflict ever since.

Therefore, water is an equivocal symbol, suggesting new life on the one hand, and death on the other. St. Paul finds in baptism a death to the world ruled by evil powers (the self-absorption which impoverishes others and oneself on the one hand or seeks *self*-justification through the Law on the other). But he also sees the possibility of rising up from the waters of chaos into the cosmos of Christ. When we "enter" Christ—the Church—there is no more fragmentation: "So there is no difference between Jews and Gentiles, between slaves and free people, between men and women; you are all one in union with Christ Jesus" (Galatians 3:28).

At the opening of Genesis, God's Spirit hovered over the chaos of the waters and, with a Word, brought forth all living

things, each in its place. Noah and his family entering the Ark,
as entering the Church, was a commitment to a new, special relationship with God; they were reborn out of the waters to begin
again. The terms of acceptance? A new respect for life. Israel
went through the tumult of the Red sea and came out the other
side a new nation, while the Egyptian slavers perished, and
finally the Israelites passed through the Jordan river into the
Promised Land. But ever after that they kept falling back into
"the slave mentality," the idols, returning to chaos.

John the Baptist appeared by that same Jordan, preaching
conversion and entry into the new Promised Land. And though
sinless himself, Jesus underwent that same baptism, going down
into the water and emerging renewed in the Holy Spirit, pictured
symbolically as a dove. This Jesus, who identified himself with
the sinners he came to save, is going to lead us from the waters
of chaos by going to the very bottom of them himself and
coming out. During his life, Jesus calmed the storm on the lake
and walked on the waters without fear.

"I have a baptism to receive, and how distressed I am until it
is over!" (Luke 12:50). For Jesus, his second baptism *was* his
death and resurrection. And the early Christian communities
knew that, because of Christ's resurrection, they too had died
and been reborn completely new:

> For surely you know that when we were baptized
> into union with Christ Jesus, we were baptized
> into union with his death. By our baptism, then,
> we were buried with him and shared his death, in
> order that, just as Christ was raised from death
> by the glorious power of the Father, so also we
> might live a new life. . . . And we know that
> our old being has been put to death with Christ

on his cross, in order that the power of the sinful self might be destroyed, so that we should no longer be the slaves of sin.

(Romans 6:3–4, 6)

Baptism "recaptures" that whole series of events. Baptism means being "plunged into" that experience of Jesus, and being born again as daughters and sons of God. "For through the living and eternal word of God you have been born again as the children of a parent who is immortal, not mortal" (1 Peter 1:23).

Anointing

In our culture, oil has a very commonplace, domestic, undramatic meaning: salads, suntans, lubrication, and it also has strongly negative associations with crude oil spills and the death of the ecology. But at the time when the sacraments were taking concrete form, oil—like water and wine—were important. Oil was what bound together the elements of bread, and therefore it symbolized the healing of fragmentation. Wrestlers anointed their entire bodies to make it more difficult for an opponent to get a hold on them, and St. Ambrose claimed that was precisely one of the functions of anointing at Christian initiation. Oil was used as soap, and also symbolically in religious rites. In the Bible, priests, monarchs, and prophets were anointed with oil when they assumed their new roles. As the first public act of Jesus' ministry, he said: "The Spirit of the Lord is upon me, because he has *anointed* me" (Luke 4:18). The word "messiah" *means* "the Anointed One." Thus, in the oil of baptism, each of us is anointed a messiah—priest, monarch, prophet:

> You are a chosen race, the King's priests, the holy
> nation, God's own people, chosen to proclaim
> the wonderful acts of God, who called you out of
> darkness into his own marvelous light.
>
> *(1 Peter 2:9)*

Note that the epistle is not speaking to officials of the
Church but to ordinary people like you. It makes no difference
if, in the ordinary secular society, they speak Greek or Hebrew,
whether they are male or female, slave or free, old or young.
They—you—are priests, prophets, peers of the Realm of God.

But—with that ever-present Christian irony—to be
anointed as priest-prophet-peer means precisely the opposite of
what it means in "the world"—not to rule but to serve:

> I appeal to you to be shepherds of the flock that
> God gave you and to take care of it willingly, as
> God wants you to, and not unwillingly. Do your
> work not for mere pay, but from a real desire to
> serve. Do not try to rule over those who have
> been put in your care, but be examples to the
> flock.
>
> *(1 Peter 5:1–3)*

Exorcism / Satan / Sin

No one can deny there is a dark side to human nature, the
element in us symbolized by the Mr. Hyde in Dr. Jekyll,
Wolfman, Dracula. The predator in us inherited from our simian
ancestors. Although our brains have a cerebral cortex capable of

writing "King Lear" and sending rockets to Jupiter, at its core is the brain stem we share with reptiles.

Just as one can have no understanding of resurrection without a felt understanding of death, or an understanding of freedom without a felt understanding of slavery, so one can have no understanding of baptism (or the whole Christian Church) without a felt understanding of evil.

But in the last half-century of our culture, we have been effectively and affectively anesthetized to evil. There is hardly a day when the papers do not announce a new civil war in some country whose name we have never heard. Pictures of starving human beings, ribs thrusting through their skins, eyes huge with hunger are so commonplace we quickly turn the page without asking, "Why? Who?" Exploitation of the poor, hatreds, rivalries, greed, manipulation of the minds of the young, drugs sold in schoolyards, drive-by shootings, families living under bridges, sexually abused children, battered and murdered wives—never get the three-inch headlines in the daily tabloids. We give as little notice to them as we do to the Kiddie Komix, unless they are especially blatant or done by a celebrity. For most, they are not evil. They are not even news.

Satan

For earlier cultures—even up to as recently as the 50s, evil was not an abstraction. It was concretized, even for the most sophisticated and educated, in the symbolic figure of Satan. Today, except for a few fringe Satan cults, that embodiment of pure evil is ludicrous to anyone who routinely flies in an airplane or uses a computer or took even elementary psychology, the stuff of "Far

Side" cartoons. Which, if there is in fact a Devil, would probably be just dandy with him.

But then for awhile there was the uncanny phenomenon of "The Exorcist." That film was different from other horror movies like "The Omen," "Nightmare on Elm Street," and even the "Exorcist" sequels, all of which gave no more real scare than the momentary terror on a roller coaster. But that film was quite different. In the first place, people were lined up for blocks (and weeks) to see it. In the second, it triggered all kinds of bizarre responses. In the third, it frightened a great many people back to some practice of religion—perhaps not for long. But at least for awhile they were aware evil does exist because they had seen it unmasked and almost palpably terrifying.

The cause of both the panic in susceptible people and the sneering condescension in sophisticated people was, once again, literalism, where the symbol *becomes* the reality. Just as it did for the marooned boys in *The Lord of the Flies* (which is a translation of the Hebrew word for demon: *Beelzebub).* They invested all the evil in themselves—the savages they became once they'd shucked the veneer of society along with their clothes—onto the pig's head on a stick and onto the mysterious entity flapping and groaning on the mountaintop. Only impractical Simon, the visionary, said, "Maybe it's only . . . us." Only he had the courage to shake off the boys' ignorant beliefs and climb the mountain to *see* that it was a dead parachutist, and when he ran down the mountain with the truth, they savaged him to death.

Generations of young people have reacted to *The Lord of the Flies* in a way less dramatic but similar to the way millions responded to "The Exorcist." There's something indefinable but *true* in there somewhere. Simon was right: "Maybe it's only . . . us." No matter how inadequate the symbol that connects us to it, moral evil exists: Auschwitz, Medellin, the South Bronx, South Central L.A., Bosnia, Rwanda, Haiti. Those are only some few of the more dramatic explosions of evil. There is wholesale evil we simply take for granted now: a million and a half abortions and millions of unwed mothers every year, fathers deserting the results of a half-hour's self-absorbed pleasure, wholesale divorce—all the inhumanities we saw before that never make the front page, the indignities we now take as merely "given." And there also are the tinier evils, which are nonetheless evil: lying to people we claim to love, cheating on a quiz that in a week we'll forget we even took, savaging the reputation of another human being in order to be "in," sneering at other people's skin, spitting gum in the drinking fountain because the basket is too far away. And their very pettiness, rather than embarrassing us, seems to exonerate us.

Quite likely there is not a literal Satan, a disembodied force that roams the world seeking to seduce us. What need would we have for such an unneeded tempter when we have a perfectly adequate one within each of us? There is no doubt whatever the reality Satan symbolizes is corrosively real, furiously active in every corner of our lives, and as easily ignored as the pollution in our rivers and the poison in our air.

Simon was right.

Many are uneasy with the exorcisms of baptism and any mention of "Satan" in the ritual. The seeming literalism of the word is a bit of embarrassment even to less sophisticated people. In the *Rite of Baptism for Children* in 1969, at the insistence of Pope Paul VI, all references to original sin were removed. But in 1973 the Congregation for the Doctrine of the Faith returned them. The problem could probably be alleviated—since it is a matter not of sacrosanct symbols but of an undeniable reality—

if the celebrant substituted for "Satan" some other formula less associated with superstitious literalism, such as "the powers within us that lead us to harm others and ourselves" or "the self-absorption and inertia we share with beasts." But there is no doubt that baptism, for adults or for infants, is a declaration that the purpose of the Church and all those genuinely within it is directly counter to that inner force.

Rite of Christian Initiation of Adults

Original Sin. There are two kinds of sin, personal sin and original sin. Of personal sin we have already said quite enough. The other question—as we saw briefly before—is: How can an infant who is incapable of any reasoned act be "guilty" of a sin committed before there was history? If within the Christian message love is more important than evil, why are we in such a hurry to get infants baptized? Vatican II's *Dogmatic Constitution on the Church* (16) makes it clear that God loves anyone born into the world, before baptism or even without baptism.

Church historians argue whether the early Church even practiced infant baptism. Rather their concept was of "family baptism," a new addition, a new microcosm of the Church. But especially under St. Augustine's view of original sin passed on through sexual intercourse, everyone human became immediately guilty of sin—even prior to personal sin. Therefore, infants "ought" to be baptized as soon as possible, lest they die and never be capable of heaven. As a result of that literalist reading, nurses and friends of the family would secretly baptize infants (whether in danger of death or not) to "insure" they would not be denied the joys of paradise.

Chapter Eight

INITIATION: CONFIRMATION

Everywhere on earth they must bear witness to Christ and give an answer to those who seek an account of that hope of eternal life which is in them. . . . Reborn as sons and daughters, they must confess before all humankind the faith which they have received from God through the Church. Bound more intimately to the Church by the sacrament of confirmation, they are endowed by the Holy Spirit with special strength. Hence they are more strictly obliged to spread and defend the faith both by word and by deed as true witnesses of Christ.

—The Constitution on the Church (10–11)

A Puzzlement

"Catechetical training is intended to make human faith become living, conscious, and active, through the light of instruction" (Vatican II, *Decree on Bishops' Pastoral Office in the Church,* 14).

What do those words really *mean* in regard to Christian faith: "living, conscious, and active"? What do they have to do with what all of us have been used to calling "religious education?" What does it all have to do with confirmation?

Confirmation of Baptism

The Church would not allow a 12-year-old girl or boy—much less a child of seven or younger—to assume a vow of celibacy. Yet in the majority of cases the Church not only allows but encourages a child before puberty to assume the responsibilities of confirmation. That truly is a puzzlement.

Baptism is a rite of passage from the strictly secular world into the Kingdom of God. Confirmation is a rite of passage from passivity to activity within that Kingdom. In primal societies, when a child entered puberty, the girl was isolated at her first menstruation (and often for the rest of her life at that time), and the shock and uncertainty was soothed by the women. In a real sense, understanding the seismic shift from childhood to adulthood is more dramatically disruptive and less easily ignored for girls, since nature lets them know, willy-nilly, that they are no longer children. For girls, physical maturity means suffering; for boys, it means an unexplainable pleasure, and as we see in our present society, that pleasure can become completely dissociated from any sense of responsibility.

Therefore, in wiser primitive societies, young boys at the time of puberty were also isolated, but in a far more terrifying way. Stranded out in the wilderness with little more than a knife, they were left for the first time to fend for themselves. Then after days of near-starvation, the men of the tribe surrounded the children, already terrified, with noise and howls. They dragged the boys to another place, and garishly painted men came yowling into the firelight, brandishing stone knives and slashing themselves. Then they circumcised the boys. The men were doing to the boys what nature had done to their sisters: made them aware that this new power in themselves was not something to be toyed with. After those nights, no boy or girl was unaware that the "whole world had changed."

Until recently, a modern boy or girl still had more than the puberty change to mystify them into realizing the "whole world had changed," at least in small ways. At confirmation, the bishop gave the recipients a slap, not hard, but still a symbol (that is gone). When you got your first pair of long pants or had your ears pierced, you had become a young man or a young woman. Now both those "rites of passage" happen before the children are potty-trained. Now there is no ethos, no myth, no rites of passage, no unwritten laws. Everything just "happens." And therefore nothing is made to seem important, even puberty.

The sacrament of confirmation is at least an opportunity to change that. In baptism, the first anointing with ordinary oil is the oil of exorcism, smeared on the chest, the medicine of strengthening. The second anointing with perfumed chrism is the oil of thanksgiving which identifies the infant with Christ, the Anointed One. This is the oil that is used in confirmation. The celebrant traces the sign of the cross with chrism on the forehead and says, "[Name], be sealed with the Gift of the Holy

Spirit." As oil bonds the elements of bread, the prayers reflect the *bonding* of the baptized with Christ and his Mystical Body, and signifies the gift of knowing not merely about Christ but knowing *Christ.* It is a sacrament both of inner growth and of external witness. Those confirmed are now "signed and sealed" with the sign of death and resurrection.

Originally, the name "confirmation" arose because the newly baptized had been led from paganism, through the waters in a pool outside the church, into Christianity, then were brought within the assembly where the bishop anointed them with chrism again and "confirmed" their baptism. The baptism with its messianic anointing had been performed by priests and deacons out of the view of the assembly, since the candidates were naked; the bishop stayed with the assembly. The second anointing was a ritual in which the official Church, through the bishop, ratified and accepted the conversion within the baptized people.

Now through an accident of history, we have a separate sacrament which gives us an opportunity for the *individual* to ratify and accept the Church—which the Church solemnizes and accepts. Not only "being confirmed" but "confirming." In confirmation one willingly assumes an active participation in the Church's apostolate, therefore there is a great deal to be said for waiting until the candidates are not only aware of what they are assuming but also are willing to assume it. The Church and individual are mutually confirming belief in one another.

Confirmation can become the sacrament of Christian maturity, which is not the same as merely "growing up" physically or even in achieving human adulthood, a personally validated conscience-psyche-soul. Children are "passive Christians." They receive Communion when they are old enough to realize that this food is not ordinary but something special: Jesus. Without the slightest understanding, their baptism and this eucharist associate them with death and resurrection, neither of which they in any way comprehend. Most are unaware death even exists.

But in adolescence young people at least *ought* to begin to be aware that they have souls, that those souls are only potential and need not be activated, that the soul is the sum and substance of who *they* are. They at least ought to be aware of the bleakness and absurdity of a life without God, without sinful or sacred, and thus the liberating function in human life of Jesus' defeat of the ultimate Gulliver, death. Only then can Christianity have any felt meaning for them. Only then can they decide if they want to be Christian.

Confirmation affirms—both on the part of the Church and on the part of the individual confirmed—a maturity *in Christ,* not merely passively baptized and attendant at Mass, but actively engaged in the apostolate. As Dr. Monika Hellwig writes:

> This goes back to a very old traditional theme which connects baptism with Easter and confirmation with Pentecost. At Easter the apostles experienced in a very vivid way the resurrection of Jesus from his terrible death. They knew then that Jesus had brought redemption into the world and that they had received that redemption, and they believed in him. It is only when we read the Pentecost story that we are told the other half of their response. In the power of the Spirit of God they then realize that they must organize themselves into a community of believers, the Church, so as to bring salvation to others.

Pentecost thus is the second foundation event to bring the Church into existence, and many call it "the birthday of the Church." Baptism is a reenactment, a recapturing, of Good Friday and Easter Sunday; confirmation is a reenactment, a recapturing of Pentecost. Baptism is a resurrection gift; confirmation is a Pentecost gift. Physical birth is the beginning of a lifetime process which at least ought to take a recognizable "shape"—character—toward the end of adolescence, though it is a process that should never end but deepen until the end of life. Similarly, baptism is the beginning of a lifetime process of growing spirituality which at least *could* reach a preliminary shape in late adolescence such that it would need a ritual like confirmation to celebrate it. But confirmation is only one way station on a lifelong journey of enriching the spirit.

Scripture

In scripture, the presence of the Holy Spirit is always an occasion of the return of cosmos from chaos, freedom from slavery, rebirth from death.

The Holy Spirit appears at the very beginning of the Bible. At the creation the breath of God broods over the waters of chaos "with ah! white wings." In the second creation story (Genesis 2), the author makes a special point concerning the creation of human beings as different from animals: God breathes his own breath into Adam. In the story of the flood (Genesis 8), God "caused a wind to blow, and the water started going down," and chaos once again yielded to cosmos. God speaks to Job from out of a whirlwind, giving Job the most difficult lesson of human life: God is not answerable to us (Job 38). God confronts the

prophet Ezekiel with a valley of dry bones (like the people of
Israel) and says:

> Mortal man, prophesy to the wind. Tell the wind
> that the Sovereign God commands it to come
> from every direction, to breathe into these dead
> bodies, and to bring them back to life.
>
> (from Ezekiel 37:9)

Luke's gospel (1:35) says Jesus was conceived by the Spirit
(the Breath) of God "resting on" his mother. At his baptism by
John in the Jordan (3:21), the soul of Jesus felt the Spirit come
down and settle upon him "like a dove." And then that same
Spirit "hurled" him into the desert to have the revelation of his
Sonship tested by the Enemy (4:1–13). Empowered by that
struggle, Jesus returned to the Nazareth synagogue and read from
the words of Isaiah: "The Spirit of God has *anointed* me" (4:18).

At the Last Supper (John 14–16), Jesus says he must die so
that his Spirit, the breath of supernatural aliveness, may be born
in them (14:16), and that Spirit will teach them not only to
remember all Jesus had said but finally to understand it (14:26),
and the Spirit will give them the courage to stand up and witness
to it no matter how intimidating the audience (15:26–27). Jesus'
death will be the climactic confrontation between God's offer of
freedom and human clinging to self-absorption. If Jesus does not
die, the spirit of prophecy will not take "possession" of them:

> It is better for you that I go away, because if I do
> not go, the Helper will not come to you. But if I
> do go away then I will send him to you. And
> when he comes, he will prove to the people of the
> world that they are wrong about sin and about

what is right and about God's judgment. The
Spirit . . . will lead you into all the truth.

(John 16:7–8, 13)

At Jesus' first appearance to the disciples, cowering in terror
of reprisals in the upper room, he says:

"Peace be with you. As the Father sent me, so I
send you." Then he breathed on them and said,
"Receive the Holy Spirit."

(John 20:21–22)

In the Acts of the Apostles, it is clear that the life-giving
Spirit of God is given to newcomers *through* his new Body, the
Church. At Pentecost (Acts 2:1–4), the Spirit took "possession"
of them, with "a noise from the sky which sounded like a strong
wind blowing" and "what looked like tongues of fire which
spread out and touched each person there." (Not just the
apostles.) It was such a startling—and transforming, empowering—experience that Peter, who had lied about knowing Jesus
on early Good Friday morning, three times, with curses, to a
waitress, immediately went outside and started preaching! The
eleven were so exhilarated the crowd thought they were drunk, at
nine in the morning! (Acts 2:15). He began quoting the prophet
Joel: "This is what I will do in the last days, God says: 'I will pour
out my Spirit on everyone.'" And what follows (Acts 2:17–39) is
about as good a summary of the gospel message as you are likely
to find anywhere.

St. Thomas Aquinas wrote that what differentiated confirmation from baptism was that, while baptism empowered one to
receive the other sacraments, confirmation provided a power to
profess one's faith in words, which according to some dissenting

modern theologians "would lead in the twentieth century, to such aberrant interpretations of confirmation as a sacrament of Catholic action or as a sacrament for the ordination of the laity." Why aberrant? It's the gospel, corroborated by the Second Vatican Council.

The rite of confirmation calls for *renewal* of the baptismal vows, this time by the individual. This time, freely. But how free can one be to assess alternatives before puberty, before the beginning of at least the invitation to think for oneself?

Two Separate Initiations

Establishing the actual practice of the sacraments of baptism and eucharist in the earliest Church is simple. But the underpinnings of the actual practice of confirmation as a *separate* sacrament in the earliest Church takes some delicate maneuvering. There is a suggestion of it when Paul met with some who had been baptized by John the Baptist. Paul said, "'The baptism of John was for those who turned from their sins; and [John] told the people of Israel to believe in the one who was coming after him—that is, in Jesus.' . . . Paul placed his hands on them, and the Holy Spirit came on them" (Acts 19:4, 6). In Acts 8:14–17, the apostles Peter and John "complete" the baptism of some Samaritans who were earlier converted and baptized "only in the name of Jesus" with an imposition of hands and the granting of the Spirit. Other than that, there is little more.

The determining factor in the separation of baptism and confirmation into two separate sacraments, quite widely separated in time, was not theological at all but merely practical (to the annoyance of sacramental theologians). During the fourth century, after the conversion of Constantine in 313, there was a significant increase in the Christian population, spread all over the countryside. It was simply impossible to have only one ritual of baptism-confirmation-first eucharist on the vigil of the Easter Mass, with the bishop present to greet the newly baptized and confirm their baptism. Nor could the people travel to the central church, nor could the bishop get to all the tiny villages even in a single year. Therefore priests continued to baptize, and later, more often infants, once most adults had been baptized. But since only a bishop could confirm, those baptized were expected to have the bishop officially confirm the baptism as soon as possible by laying on of hands and anointing with chrism, either in a pilgrimage to the central church or on the bishop's infrequent visits.

At the moment, that is the way things stand, and the separation of the sacraments of initiation is a source of irritation for sacramental theologians since it destroys the "neatness" of logical progression from conversion from the world's values in baptism, to the Church's confirmation of that conversion, and only then into full participation in the eucharist which embodies the reality of the People of God. (Which has been reinstituted in the new *Rite of Christian Initiation for Adults.*) Thus confirmation is a sacrament in search of a theology. Perhaps at least a clue is available if we accept that sometimes "logical" is not as important as "psychological."

However the sacraments came to be separated, we do have the separate sacrament of confirmation now and have for centuries. What's more, it is a splendid opportunity to invite young people to a personal conversion.

A Rite of Passage at Puberty

For all our theologizing on the nature and meaning of confirmation and its most "fitting" place in the scheme of Christian initiation, we could allow the whole complex of problems involved in puberty to help us understand the *human* element that dramatic physical and psychological change could add to confirmation.

Puberty is a rite of passage over which we have no physical control, but the whole purpose of adolescence in human development is that the persons suffering it need to grow psychologically as well as physically, into personally apprehended and accepted *selves.* Human maturity doesn't "kick on" with the onset of sexual potency nor with the issuance of a college diploma; it is rather a gradual *process* as slow and gradual as the process of an infant learning muscle control. Everything is *changed;* it's a whole different world—or at least it's enormously different from what I thought it was. How do I deal with it? Where's a compass? Psychologists Carl Jung and Erik Erikson could offer us a great deal of insight in finding a theology of confirmation.

Puberty is not merely a sexual or even physical change. This former child now has to begin taking on newer, more demanding roles to prepare to enter a far larger community than the family or school, to begin making a living, to prepare for intimacy and partnership, to prepare for parenthood. Puberty is a time when our bodies tell us we have been newly empowered in a very intimidating but fascinating way. That very physical change is one more *invitation:* to adult responsibility. If confirmation could be somehow mortised into that natural process, we might take young people beyond an awareness of responsibility to the human community to a deeper sense of apostleship in the Church which tries to de-paganize and invigorate that community with the liberation of the sons and daughters of God.

Such a process could begin at the outset of puberty, in a completely natural (not supernatural) way, a time in which older men and women could meet separately with boys and girls and simply "let their hair down" about sexuality, its problems, its challenges, its enrichment. That preliminary offer of service is too early to attempt at a spiritual dimension, since precisely because of those physical changes, young people are at a time in their lives when they are most self-absorbed and alienated.

That service of the Church would help young people drop the self-protective barriers of brashness or shyness, to feel at "home," not only with their new selves but with the Church as "Mother," especially for the increasing number of children from dysfunctional families. Moreover, such an initial attempt to let young people know the Church "understands" would form a basis for a later probing of adulthood in the Church, at an age when they are beginning to question, able to cope with "Macbeth" and trigonometry: a catechesis for confirmation *as* adult Catholics. But first they have to *experience* a real identification with a serving community if confirmation and commitment to that community are to make any sense. Grace builds on nature. You have to plow before you plant.

Especially with youngsters who don't attend religious schools, the Church could make itself more appealing as a life-giving myth meaningful *to the young person* if it began to deal with the felt problems everyone faces going through adolescence, human problems, before dealing with the transcendent: inadequacy, the meaninglessness of the lessons day after day, fear of others' judgments, jealousy, sexuality, commitment. "Why is fulfillment always in the *future?*"

We can help them understand their parents as equally fragile, equally limited, equally needful of enlightenment. That would be a first step toward an apostolate. If we can't make them vulnerable even to people they claim to love, we will have little luck getting them to care for strangers. But if they began to feel that the Church is a place that holds wisdom, savvy, a genial peace with the way ordinary human life is, we might purchase credibility for the gospel. At the moment, not many feel that is true.

Age of Confirmation

What was once a single ritual for adults became the separate rituals of baptism, confirmation, and first communion, widely separated in one's lifetime. That integration of initiation has been reinstituted in the *Rite of Christian Initiation for Adults.* After much instruction and testing, adult catechumens are once again baptized outside the Church gathering, welcomed inside to be confirmed by the bishop (or in some cases a priest), then invited to participate in their first eucharist. Such a practice avoids the theological unfitness of confirmation "conferring the Holy Spirit" when the candidate has already received the Holy Spirit at baptism. Explaining what confirmation adds to what baptism has already done requires a bit of theological dancing. Further, it seems to some to use confirmation only as a catechetical "carrot" to keep kids going to religion classes.

Those who object to a delay of confirmation argue that the rite could seem to have changed from the ritualization of a prior conversion to an attempt to bring about conversion. The point of this chapter is precisely that: confirmation as a vehicle for adult acceptance of baptism in the already baptized.

Unfortunately, as with other liturgical innovations, such reluctance is an example of sound theology defying sound psychology. As with teaching the Trinity to young people still incapable of "Macbeth" or trigonometry, academic rightness about the proper age for confirmation tyrannizes over the day-to-day, jutjaw-to-jutjaw experience of those who have not only to explain the faith but make their truculent audiences want to interiorize a need for it. First, children of twelve are simply not psychologically ready either for confirmation or for the Trinity. Many—one would risk saying most—have been baptized but never had a conversion experience. Second, children of twelve, in our almost totally secularized culture, are dramatically less able than children brought up in a culture suffused with religion—primitive, medieval, or till recently modern Judaeo-Christian.

"The Age of Reason"

In *The Rite of Christian Initiation for Adults*, (par. 1) infants are defined as children before the age of reason, that is "those who have not reached the age of discernment and therefore cannot have or profess personal faith." Traditionally, that opening of the specific human potential has been fixed around age seven, and it was based simply on the fact that at that age a child begins personally to know when he or she has done something "wrong." However, it doesn't seem to have taken into consideration the difference between knowing that some action is *disapproved of* by parents or a particular society and *internalizing the reasons why* that action is dehumanizing, adopting it into one's personally validated moral code.

Anyone who says the age of reason "clicks on" at age seven has never taught high-school sophomores.

You can't make genuine converts out of children. Those who want to return to the integral Roman rite of baptism-confirmation-first communion should consider, first, that the rite was formulated when most of the candidates for that rite were adults and, second, that the rite "worked" for them but does not "work" for us and, third, that we have had two separated sacraments for the last thousand-plus years. History and theology have no effect if they spurn the psychology of the recipients.

Furthermore, equating the ability to reason with the ability to make an act of faith in an invisible God is quite simplistic. One can have exhaustive knowledge about the reasons to believe and still disbelieve—or simply be so caught up in the joys of newly adult bodies not to care one way or the other.

"The Age of Reason" in a Pagan Culture

Furthermore, beyond faith in God, the gospel demands a complete reversal of the "values" young people today have been led to believe are simply givens, beyond question. At the age of seven, a child has not yet even begun puberty; he or she may have a streetwise savvy about sexuality but has never known the quantum difference between knowledge of sex and experiencing it. They would not be allowed to take vows of celibacy at that age.

If religious education focuses on conversion—rather than merely ingesting data and passing tests—the first and greatest task is to try to *de-paganize*. Till then, the gospel, the Church, and every one of the sacraments have no chance whatever.

It was far easier to be Christian when the entire society around you was at least nominally Christian, professing the same values, worshipping fairly frequently and in at least similar manner. Jews shared the same basic, altruistic and God-centered values and embodied them in ritual practice. Although there were interpersonal and interfaith raw points, all Western lives were governed by the same values: uprightness, honesty, thrift, fairness, neighborliness—up until as recently as the 1950s. Things were not as serene as a Norman Rockwell painting, but in general we all belonged to a common, altruistic ethos.

In the half-century since then, however, that ethos has gone topsy-turvy. If a youngster from that era—even a juvenile delinquent—could somehow be transported to today, he or she would be flabbergasted, not just at the newfangled gadgets but at the complete overturning of values even they respected. The media in every way, programs to commercials to MTV, have transformed greed and lust from objectionable vices to admirable virtues. Doris-Day virginity is an embarrassment. The basic goal of life is not substance but appearance. "Success" no longer means living a life to be proud of but getting as much as one can as soon as one can: money, fame, sex, and power. Even the Bowery Boys and the Dead End Kids would be shocked. So-called "values" and behavior even they would have shunned we now take as not only acceptable but commonplace.

To ask for adult baptism today—or to ask for adult confirmation of one's baptism—takes a great deal of conversion, since the gospel that baptism testifies to is a 180-degree turnabout from the values that permeate our society and saturate young peoples' personal value systems.

Those undergoing conversion have to learn to perceive, think, and evaluate in a way radically different from that to which they have become accustomed. While the central symbols of the baptismal rite—water, oil, and touching—are symbols found in other religions, they are also culturally conditioned by a 2000-year Christian tradition. Today, even as *natural* symbols they are foreign to many young people whose only contact with water is in pipes and pools, whose only experience of oil is for salads and suntans, and who treat touching as an intrusion or an approach.

Confirmation and the Adult Rite

Confirmation should not be used as a catechetical carrot—which, at best remains effective only until no later than junior high school if the age-12 custom remains. Rather than trying to "nab" them with confirmation before they can "get away," like baptizing infants instantly so premature death will not condemn them to Limbo, why not wait for confirmation—just as for the triple sacraments conferred at the end of RCIA—until the individual *wants* to be confirmed because he or she has in fact had an adult conversion? Why not find ways to induce that conversion during the latter years of high school and in college campus ministry? A young person without confirmation is still baptized and can still live an exemplary life. But if confirmation followed a genuine personal conversion, we would have more lifelong active apostles.

The 1983 Code of Canon Law states: "The sacrament of confirmation is to be conferred on the faithful at about the age of discretion unless the conference of bishops determines another age" (891). Usually, children are confirmed around age 12, thus ordinarily before the onset of puberty, at least in males. Since then, many countries have postponed confirmation still further. The National Council of Catholic Bishops has not stipulated an age, allowing local bishops to decide.

Objections to Delay

A strong contrary position is posed consistently in the many excellent entries in *The New Dictionary of Sacramental Worship* (Fink, ed., Liturgical Press, 1990).

"It lost some of its initiation character." For whom? Surely not for the recipients. Confirmation for the born Catholic, even at age twelve, is a far more importantly felt rite than baptism was for an infant. "Today, theological understanding of confirmation seeks to restore it again as an *initiation* sacrament intimately related to baptism." For whom? Not for a child who has no felt awareness of death and therefore not of resurrection, and therefore no ability to understand being invited by baptism "into Christ's death and resurrection."

One is tempted to believe most lifelong Catholics have no real understanding of that massive truth, partly because, although it was surely prepared for, confirmation could have received far more intense preparation, partly because that preparation carefully avoided any connection with puberty and therefore a totally different role in the Church community, and most importantly because that preparation had far more to do with ingestion and testing of theological data and far less to do with conversion of heart and a complete turnabout of priorities.

Unfortunately, while confirmation at about seven years of age is affirmed as the general practice of the Latin church, the possibility of deferring the rite until "the recipients are more mature" is still admitted. This not only destroys the initiatory sequence and makes its theological unity more obscure; it effectively changes the emphasis of confirmation from the perfection of baptism through the reception of the Holy Spirit to a personal ratification of the candidates' baptismal faith. While it may be argued that the creation of such a rite is pastorally desirable, confirmation should not be asked to play that role (610).

Why not? The argument is theologically unchallengeable, and yet it not only denies the receptivities of candidates so young, but more importantly it misses a golden opportunity to evoke adult conversion at a later age—which seems far more desirable than theological nicety.

Confirmation often is depicted as a rite of passage, a maturity sacrament, the "completion" of initiation; each explanation lacks compelling justification in tradition, and inadvertently suggests that infant baptism is deficient, and/or confirmation is somehow more significant than eucharist (271).

But what about confirmation's significance *not* to the sacramental theologian but to the *recipient?* The tradition means nothing to him or her, really, only to the theologian. No candidate for confirmation ever expressed a feeling that confirmation was somehow "lessening" the meaning of baptism. Rather, for many, it was the first time in their lives they ever really questioned what baptism had meant in the first place!

> [The separated rite] calls for great sensitivity, to avoid giving the impression that the Spirit is now being conferred for the first time, or that this is the way Catholics ratify their baptismal vows, or that this is the sacrament of adolescent strengthening or of Catholic action or of the "ordination of the laity!" None of these pious explanations parading as theology has advanced our knowledge or practice of confirmation or been, for that matter, a healthy development (285).

Healthy for whom? Of course the Spirit is not conferred on the recipients for the first time. The first time they experienced the grace of God was conception, even before baptism. Nonbelievers are being visited by grace all the time. And this *is*—or at least could be—a time when a Catholic personally ratifies a choice made for him or her before they could reason. And at least according to Vatican II, baptism and confirmation *are* an invitation to apostolate ("Catholic action") and an "ordination of the laity," which was proclaimed in 1 Peter 2:9:

> You are the chosen race, the King's priests, God's own people, chosen to proclaim the wonderful acts of God, who called you out of darkness into his own marvelous light.

Insights from the Adult Rite
of Conversion

If a parish had begun with adults and young people reflecting together on the problems and joys of their new sexuality, there would already be a basis for the young people's belief that the Church was "home," a place to figure out problems and find some meaning for the fragments of their lives. If the children's baptismal godparents were to go through that earlier process with them, so much the better. That same godparent could be the young person's guide and sponsor through the process of preparation for confirmation, and in the process revivify his or her own faith. It would certainly make the request at baptism a genuine lifetime commitment on the part of the godparent to be part of this infant's Christian maturation rather than just "being there."

The process of preparation for confirmation could mirror the periods of the Adult Rite: first a period, or stage, of inquiry in which the candidate and his or her sponsor sit and talk, one-on-one, about the fact that the young person just might be missing out on a very important dimension of human life: the transcendent. They could mull over together the readings for each Sunday's Mass, puzzling over how these insights could enrich the life of a person today, living in a pagan culture. Then, as with the Adult Rite, sponsors and candidates would come forward during Mass for a Rite of Acceptance, in which the sponsor testifies to the candidate's worthiness and the two write their names in the registry of those accepted for more intense preparation.

The second period, or stage, would parallel the catechumenate, a time of formation with other candidates and sponsors and the parish team: reading, discussing, probing together the heart (not just the mind) of the gospel and including a period of active service. On Trinity Sunday, as with adults in the rite of acceptance into the order of catechumens, those requesting confirmation and their sponsors could enact the same rite in which the sponsor signs with a cross the senses of the candidate and the celebrant welcomes them to the group to be confirmed at Pentecost. They should be led to understand that the seven gifts of the Holy Spirit given in confirmation—knowledge, understanding, wisdom, prudence, courage, reverence, and awe of God—are not gifts in the worldly sense. Rather like all gifts of love, undeserved, they are challenges to activate those powers in one's life.

The final weekend, paralleling the initiation of young people into a new adult role in tribal communities, there could be a three-day retreat for candidates and sponsors, concluding with the Mass of confirmation. As the Adult Rite takes place on Easter, let confirmation take place on Pentecost, even without a bishop, since priests can be delegated to confirm. Moreover, it is the Church which ratifies this choice, and the Church is in the pews, and let them witness their approval with applause. And at the sacrament itself, let the music be *their* music, perhaps written by themselves during the formation period.

As with the baptism of an adult, confirmation ought to reflect a conversion. Like adult converts, those to be confirmed need a growing awareness that the gospel revelation about the dimensions of human life is *true* and *internalized*. In the process, they ought to experience a genuine sense of belonging. They ought to *feel* freer. (Can I see your freedom? Can I feel your joy?) The sacraments are surely not magic, but they ought to *feel* magical! And all concerned should realize throughout the process this is not just preparing candidates to *be* confirmed but to *confirm*. It is not just a commission but a commitment.

Such a process would change the whole emphasis of catechesis from merely imparting information usually forgotten before the last test is finished to genuine evangelization and an invitation to personal conversion. It could also be a challenge for college campus ministry. Like the Adult Rite, preparation for confirmation ought to be (at least) a year-long process, a journey between extremes, darkness and light, slavery and freedom, falsehood and truth, death and life.

To be genuine, confirmation cannot be a treadmill onto which one is "expected" to climb at a certain age because all of the other boys and girls are doing it. It has to be a reasoned, free choice. In adolescence young people can be invited to the world of adult responsibilities and commitments. But they can't become adult unless free to make their own commitments. That means they may choose to make no commitments for awhile, which is perfectly legitimate, provided they don't make a lifetime of it like the people on "Cheers." That also means they may make commitments contrary to the ones that have given meaning to their parents' lives. But love is not love unless it is freely given.

Chapter Nine

HEALING: FORGIVENESS

For by our interior qualities, each of us outstrips the whole sum of mere things. We find reenforcement in this profound insight whenever we enter into our own hearts. God, who probes the heart, awaits us there. There we discern our proper destiny beneath the eyes of God. Thus, when human beings recognize in themselves a spiritual and immortal soul, they are not being mocked by a deceptive fantasy springing from mere physical or social influence. On the contrary, we are getting to the depths of the very truth of the matter. —The Church Today (14)

A Puzzlement

In *The Great Divorce,* C. S. Lewis's fantasy about heaven, travelers from purgatory to the fields outside heaven are invited to come in. Only one thing they cannot bring with them: their self-absorption. For many, that is too precious to surrender, so they get back on the bus and return to the dull grey town which is purgatory and now, for them, hell: "Better to reign in hell than serve in heaven."

One boy has a lizard on his shoulder, whispering, whispering. The boy cringes at what he hears, yet he is fascinated by it. One of the heavenly creatures asks if the boy wants him to kill it, but the boy shrugs and says, "Oh, no. See. He's quite quiet now." A second time the heavenly personage asks, the boy curses at him: "Why can't you just creep up and kill it without my knowing!" Finally, the wretched boy screams, "Yes! Yes, *kill* it!" The shining person grasps the lizard and crushes it, throwing it down and breaking its back.

But the body begins to shimmer and grow, and the lizard transforms into a great white stallion! And the boy leaps on the stallion's back and rides whooping through the fields into heaven.

What is the lizard? What is the stallion?

What Is Sin?

Just as we can never appreciate resurrection without a felt awareness of death, just as we can never appreciate freedom without a felt awareness of slavery, we can never appreciate the liberation of the sacrament of reconciliation without a felt awareness of alienation, fragmentation, sin. Sin is a sense that things are out of kilter, that I'm not really OK as a person, that I am no longer at "home."

Today, it is commonplace to close our minds to anything that might turn into a "guilt trip." Yet that sense of guilt (when the cause is undeniably real) is a very healthy human feeling, like hunger in our bellies that keeps us alive. It is a hunger in the mistreated soul that urges us to make things right again. The healthy soul turns guilt into responsibility, first by acknowledging it, then by admitting it openly, and then by doing something to change our deadening habits. As we saw in the first chapter, what you have in a world without sinful or sacred—without guilt—is Auschwitz, gang rapes, pushers, saturation bombing, toxic waste dumps, terrorists. It is undeniable that what our society desperately needs is to stop suppressing legitimate guilt and turn it into responsibility.

Although we frequently use the two terms interchangeably, there is a significant difference between moral evil and sin. Even good atheists who have no belief in "sin," are well aware of the prevalence of moral (human) evil. Leaving God for the moment out of the background against which we measure ourselves, we can see that there still is an objective web of relationships between each of us and the whole physical planet we share: the physical ecology. If any one of us violates that web—by shooting poison into the atmosphere, spewing chemicals into rivers, defacing walls with graffiti, or even throwing a single hamburger box out a car window, we are all eventually going to pay, even the perpetrators: an ugly, deadened, deadly world. Just so, there is also an objective web of relationships between each of us and all the *human* inhabitants with whom we share the planet: a moral (human) ecology. If any one of us violates that web—by holding human beings in slavery, allowing them to starve in agony, raping or murdering or assaulting them, insulting them with noise, or even by lying to them, we are all eventually going to pay: a world in which no one can trust anyone else.

If morality (without any reference to religion) means simply what we have to do to consider ourselves decent human beings, any child is capable of moral evil, which violates the "horizontal" web of relationships we have with all human beings. But strictly speaking, it may not be a "sin," because sin further violates the "vertical" relationship we have to the One who created us. If that personal relationship with God doesn't exist, one may not (strictly speaking) have knowingly committed sin. But one is still guilty of moral evil.

Sin is also an offense against oneself, in which we curtail our own freedom and gradually weigh ourselves down with the anchors of habit. It changes our personalities—and by that very fact affects the people who care for us. Every sin is a failure to become what we might have been, and gradually it corrodes our ability to be that fullest self. Our self-absorption becomes almost literal: we devour ourselves till there is no self left. Oscar Wilde shows it dramatically in his story, *The Picture of Dorian Gray*, in which a handsome and gifted young man gives himself over to a life of self-indulgence, degrading women, exploiting others' weaknesses, defrauding his friends. But one day he notices that his portrait over the fireplace looks a bit different, and as the weeks go by it becomes so obviously shriveled and deformed that he has to hide it in the attic, where it continues to mirror his true corrupted soul.

"Sin" is one of the most basic terms in the Christian vocabulary, as common as "grace" or "God," because sin really means being *out of* a relationship with God, being "disconnected." The Church not only preaches penitence but promises forgiveness for that disconnectedness. As we have seen so often before, there is unarguably a "dark side" to human nature. On the one hand, being scrupulously aware of that dark side can lead to despair; on the other, being defensively unaware of it can lead to a life of triviality and illusion. The Greek word for sin is *harmatia,* an archery term for "missing the mark." Not just making an error in judgment in a particular case, but missing the whole point of human life; not just a violation of a law but an insult to a friendship with the One to whom we owe existence—and all the gifts that followed from that first one; not just a servant's failure to carry out a master's orders, but the ingratitude of a child to its parent.

The *state* of sin is a state of an enslaved consciousness, a surrender of freedom, and one can get real insight into its nature from comparing it to chemical addiction. Like habituation to drugs, habituation to sin causes hardening of the heart so that, as Carson McCullers said, the heart grows pitted and tough like the seed of a peach. Like drugs, sin becomes an unshakable habit, so that every next time makes sin easier. And the indifferent sinner "dies" as a human being, just as addicts do, because one's best self never has a chance to be born.

The continued *state* of either "sin" or "grace," is what theologians today call the *"fundamental option,"* a matter of one's whole *basic disposition* to God. It is rooted at the depth of the self—the soul, and determines the overall pattern and choices of one's life. Hitler and mob hitmen clearly have a fundamental option quite different from that of Thomas More and Mother Teresa. They are in two races moving 180-degrees opposite to one another. None of us believes he or she is as wicked as Hitler or as holy as Thomas More. The crucial question is: Which direction are you running?

It's worth noting, too, that the position most deadly to the good is not evil; the most lethal position is utter indifference. As

God says in the book of Revelation: "I know that you are neither
cold nor hot. How I wish you were either one or the other! But
because you are lukewarm, neither hot nor cold, I am going to
spit you out of my mouth!" (3:15–16).

In light of what we saw when considering original sin, Sean
Fagin, S. M., says: "The third chapter of Genesis tells us nothing
about what happened at the beginning of time, but . . . it is a
story to explain what is happening *all* of the time." A skeletal
sketch which every sin since has duplicated: human self-absorption, the arrogance which believes I can get along without God;
I can determine what is right and wrong, despite the quite
explicit purposes written by God right into the natures of rocks,
vegetables, animals, and human beings. We become blinded by
self-interest, and in those rare honest moments when we do open
our eyes, we realize we are "naked" and helpless. Not only have
we turned away from God; we no longer feel at "home" even
with ourselves or with our neighbors. Even then, like Adam, we
resort to excuses: "The woman *you* put here with me gave me the
fruit, and I ate it" (Genesis 3:12). [Author's italics] How often
has each of us resorted to the same kind of scapegoating? The
Genesis event never actually happened. And yet it happens
uncountable times every day. It may be a mythical story, but it
tells the whole psychology of sin.

As George McCauley, S.J., puts it: "The sacrament of
penance is . . . a conversation between Christians about sin."
Something very salutary in us wants to talk about the way we've
used and misused our freedom. "This human need is attested to
by groups as diverse as bartenders and psychiatrists." But sitting
or kneeling to confess doesn't wipe out the scapegoating; we grow
afraid; we hedge. "We quickly become expert at hiding our true
selves behind words. We dissemble with them; we throw up

verbal roadblocks which delay entrance into the private citadel of our thoughts. With words we put people off and we lead them on. We pick and choose from among our meager treasure of words to find those which best ornament our pale souls."

That is what the sacrament of reconciliation is for: complete honesty with oneself, to *submit* to the truth, to be humbled into freedom. Through that honesty, we can begin to transform the power of our vices into the grace of God's aliveness, like the lizard becoming the stallion, to carry us—not into heaven—but into a life which makes sense again, where we're OK, at "home."

When we approach the sacrament of forgiveness, we take one liberating step away from self-deception: we become not just the observers of our weakness, but its accusers. We move beyond admission of guilt, beyond even recognition of a need for forgiveness; we now desire to be *whole* again.

Jesus and Personal Confession

Jesus never waxed wroth over a sexual sinner. In fact, sexual sins didn't seem very high on Jesus' priority list. Surely not as high as they have been in the eyes of the official Church, owing to the intervention of Plato, St. Augustine, and others. Incandescent minds, but they were not Jesus.

Nor was Jesus irate at Judas's impending treachery; in fact he washed Judas's feet (John 13:12), and in the moment before his arrest said, "Be quick about it, friend!" (Matthew 26:50). He didn't revile Peter for his triple cowardice, he merely asked— three times—"Simon son of John, do you love me?" (John 21:15–17). He didn't consider wealth a sin; he loved the rich young man, even unable to sell all; Lazarus and his family seemed comfortable; Jesus made no complaint that Zacchaeus gave away "only" half his ill-gotten goods; a penniless Samaritan was no help for the victim in the ditch, and if Joseph of Arimathea had not been wealthy, Jesus would have gone unburied. He seemed none too cautious for the niceties of Sabbath observance (Mark 2:27) or about enjoying food and wine; in fact, his enemies accused him of being "a glutton and wine drinker" (Luke 7:34). Even "heretics" had gentler treatment from Jesus than they could expect from the later traditional Church; according to the parable of the weeds (Matthew 13:24–30), they should be left as they are until the harvest.

In fact, the only sinners who upset Jesus—strongly—were the clergy and Temple minions! He reacted fiercely to the hypocrisy and grandstanding of the pharisees, resorting to some rather insulting (not to mention imprudent) terms: "Frauds," "blind fools," "hypocrites," "blind guides," "vipers' nests" (Matthew 23). And one can almost hear Jesus grind his teeth confronting the thickheaded materialism of his own twelve seminarians. What is common to these offenses is their consistent refusal to see anything wrong with their suppositions, no sense of a need for repentance, since the rectitude of their convictions was unquestionable to them.

Oh, Jesus mentions sins aplenty: fornication, theft, murder, adultery, greed, maliciousness, deceit, sensuality, envy, blasphemy, arrogance, an obtuse spirit. He was not as blasé about sin as many nominal Christians like to believe he was. But perhaps the root sin is the last in his list, an obtuse spirit: the self-absorption which refuses to admit one did wrong and the inertia which finds it too much effort and embarrassment to go back to the first wrong turn and start over.

But Jesus also offered forgiveness aplenty. When Peter asked how many times we must forgive, Jesus told him "seventy times seven" times, and if God expects as much of us, we can expect at least as much of God. Though sinless himself, Jesus had a remarkable empathy for weakness. Quoting Isaiah, he said, "He will not break off a bent reed, nor put out a flickering lamp" (Matthew 12:20). "I assure you that people can be forgiven all their sins and all the evil things they may say. But whoever says evil things against the Holy Spirit will never be forgiven, because [that person] has committed an eternal sin" (Mark 3:28–29). Perhaps that puzzling, sole unforgivable sin is despair, but a case could also be made for its being "an obtuse spirit," impregnable even to the Spirit's movement suggesting something is amiss and needs forgiving.

Unconditional love and forgiveness of debts is difficult for us to comprehend. Even catechesis (still) opts for the economic metaphor: a God so ego-bruised by Adam and Eve there could be no love from God till every last shekel of ransom was paid in the blood of Jesus. Which is, however well-intentioned, blasphemous. God loves us as helplessly as a mother loves her child on death row. Our sins do nothing to God; their effects are in *us,* even though we refuse to see them as self-servingly as Dorian Gray.

The key—as so many gospel parables show—is opening the eyes, submitting to the cure of our blindness. Jesus did not come to hawk guilt; he came to offer freedom. As he said in his inauguration "platform" in the Nazareth synagogue, he was sent to declare the Year of God (Luke 4:16–19): unconditional amnesty for those willing to *avail* themselves of it. As the four episodes we will consider here prove conclusively, in no single case was there need to crawl, to vacuum the soul of every peccadillo, to submit to a retaliatory penance—much less "the temporal punishment due to sin" even after an all-merciful God has forgiven. Unconditional amnesty. The only requisite—in the moral practice of Jesus—was admitting one's *need* of forgiveness.

The Woman Known as a Sinner
(Luke 7:36–50)

Simon the Pharisee had invited Jesus to dinner, though Simon forgot or forbore the courtesy of offering his guest a greeting kiss, water to wash his feet, and oil to anoint his brow. As they dined, a woman "known in the town to be a sinner" entered, stood behind Jesus' couch, weeping. She wiped the tears from Jesus' feet with her hair, kissing them and anointing them with oil. Simon fumed; if Jesus were a prophet, he'd know what kind of woman this was. His rectitude was at stake, not her shame. But Jesus pointed to the woman: she, a known sinner, had done for him everything the upright pharisee had failed to do. "I tell you, then, the great love she has shown proves that her many sins have been forgiven. But whoever has been forgiven little shows only a little love" (Luke 7:47). The woman said nothing. No careful catalogue of sins; no pleading. She merely came to Jesus and humbled herself. And all her unspoken sins were forgiven. Jesus said nothing about restitution or atonement. "Your sins are forgiven." Period.

The Adulterous Woman
(John 8:1–11)

As Jesus was teaching in the Temple, pharisees brought a woman who had been caught in adultery. (Nothing said of her consort.) According to Mosaic law, she should be stoned; what did *he* say? Jesus merely bent and began tracing in the dirt. When they persisted, he said, "Whichever one of you has committed no sin may throw the first stone at her" (John 8:7). And he bent back to his puzzling tracery. Gradually, the accusers drifted away, leaving only Jesus and the woman. He finally looked up and said, "Where are they? Is there no one left to condemn you?" She replied, "No one, sir." And Jesus said, "Well then, I do not condemn you either. Go, but do not sin again."

Again, no questions like the ones priests were once taught to ask routinely: "What caused this? Are there problems in your marriage? Are there any other sins? And the sins of your past life?" No homilies, and surely no anger—only quiet acceptance and the admonition to avoid doing it again.

The Samaritan Woman
(John 4:4–40)

On a journey through Samaria, Jesus stopped at the Well of Shechem and sent his disciples to the village for provisions. A Samaritan woman came to draw water and expressed surprise that he, a Jew, would ask water of a Samaritan. Jesus said, "If you only knew what God gives and who it is that is asking you for a drink, you would ask him, and he would give you life-giving water" (John 4:10). Again, a matter of seeing, not only through mindless prejudice but the invitation to a freer, richer life.

There was an easy, teasing banter between them, playing on the idea of the water in her well and water which gave eternal life. When Jesus asked her to call her husband, she answered forthrightly, "I don't have a husband." And he replied (surely with a grin), "You are right when you say you don't have a husband. You have been married to five men, and the man you live with now is not really your husband. You have told me the truth" (4:18). But Jesus did not pursue her multiple sexual unions. Instead, he spoke about something more important, a time when, soon, "authentic worshipers will worship the Father in Spirit and truth." At that the woman ran to gather the villagers. And when the disciples returned and begged Jesus to eat, he replied, "I have food to eat that you know nothing about" (4:32). Any confessor who has set a penitent free knows that repletion.

The Prodigal Father
(Luke 15:11–32)

The clearest insight into Jesus' (and God's—and therefore our) treatment of sinners is this story. The only character in both parts is the father, the one the Storyteller wanted his audience to identify with. Note the details.

When the younger son demanded "his share" of the estate, the father did not say, "*What? It's my* estate that I've worked a lifetime for!" Instead, he gave it, as unhesitatingly as God gives us life, without strings, unconditionally, to do with what we choose, even against the divine will.

When the boy had frittered it away, reduced to feeding swine, he saw his mistake and headed for home, making up a memorized confession. But the father saw him "a long way off . . . and was deeply moved." Which implies the father was out there every day, hoping. And the father ran to the boy, not the other way round, threw his arms around him and kissed him—*before* the boy could apologize! The boy got only the first sentence of his speech out before his father hushed him and calling to his servants said: "Hurry! Bring the best robe and put it on him. Put a ring on his finger and shoes on his feet. Then go and get the prize calf and kill it, and let us celebrate with a feast!

For this son of mine was dead, but now he is alive; he was lost, but now he has been found" (Luke 15:22–24).

The father did not say, "I want an account of every shekel before you get back into this house!" Nothing of the shame the boy had caused him, because at the moment the boy's shame was more important than his own. Not a penance but a *party!* Because the lost sheep had found his way home. The whole gospel.

But there was another son, just as blind and perhaps farther from "home" than the profligate had ever been. He found the cause of the merriment and slumped into a sulk. But notice again the father came out *to* the son because the son refused to come in and celebrate his brother's rebirth. The older boy could think only of what he had done for his father, forgetting that, without his father, he would never have existed. Like so many, he had tried to merit the love his father had already felt for him nine months before he had ever seen the boy's face. His self-absorption and self-righteousness had blinded him to the whole point.

A Matter of Emphasis

Jesus does talk of punishment. The God he pictured and embodied is not a Cosmic Patsy who forgives anything, even when we have no inclination to apologize. The key to Jesus' moral practice—in every case, without exception—does involve the humility to admit one has wandered, and to come home.

But of the nearly 4,000 verses in the gospels, Jesus speaks of hell in Mark only once, in Luke three times, in Matthew six times, in John not at all. He speaks of judgment in Mark only once, in Luke twice, in Matthew and John six times each. In his lengthiest consideration of judgment (Matthew 25:31–46), the crucial question pivots on none of the sins Jesus mentioned (fornication, theft, murder, adultery, etc.) but on the sole issue of one's sensitivity or obtuseness to the suffering of Jesus in the hungry, the thirsty, the imprisoned.

Contrast the relative rareness of Jesus speaking about hell or judgment with the profusion of times in the gospels when he both spoke and acted as one come to heal and to forgive, and you come away with a picture of Christian moral practice which is far different from what many Christians have come to expect.

There is no doubt we sin. There is no doubt we too often blithely slither off the hook and become amnesiac about our faults. But there is also no doubt that, according to Jesus, being forgiven ought to be a great deal easier than we fear.

We cannot emphasize too strongly that our sins do no harm to God, only to our own souls. God is God simply because God *can't* be offended! If the notion makes any sense at all it is that we *try* to offend God; and it just won't work and we end up offending ourselves. In the gospel, God does not uproot the weeds, but allows them to stay till the harvest. God gives us freedom—which is something we find terribly difficult to give to one another.

Once again, we have to beware becoming prisoners of our metaphors. Pictures of the Last Judgment are very much colored by references back to the Old Testament Day of Yahweh, a day of wrath. But we forget that Jesus came precisely to set us free of that image of God: God is *Abba,* "Papa." On the other hand, we can't overemphasize that metaphor either, making God no more judgmental than a doting Grandpa. In the Judgment Jesus envisions, the sole question (Matthew 25) will be about how compassionate—how forgiving and merciful—we were

ourselves. In a very real sense, it will not be God judging us, but
our finally seeing ourselves against the background of God and
judging ourselves. As Jesus says in John's gospel:

> For God did not send his son into the world to
> be its judge, but to be its savior. Those who
> believe in the Son are not judged; but those who
> do not believe have already been judged, because
> they have not believed in God's only Son. This is
> how the judgment works: the light has come into
> the world, but people love the darkness rather
> than the light (3:17–19).

Penance in Church History

It is clear that Jesus did forgive sinners one-on-one, just as we do
today in the rite of reconciliation. But in the early Church,
baptism was the principal means of redemption from sin, and
the eucharist was the weekly means to sustain conversion. There
does not seem any evidence at all of a ritual by which individuals
could periodically be honest with themselves, the Church, and
God and receive absolution.

Ancient: First to Sixth Centuries

During the second century of the Church's existence, a question
arose whether someone, whose notorious public sins had
excluded him or her from the Church, could be rebaptized. The
main such sins were idolatry, apostasy, murder, abortion and

publicly flaunted adultery. But baptism was the Church's commitment to sinners and, like the fidelity of God, can't be taken away, even though they had cut themselves off from communion. Instead, the Church gave the person a public penance (wearing burlap, kneeling outside the church door during the eucharist), so that he or she could demonstrate not only to everybody else but to *themselves* they had changed, and then they had a ritual ceremony in which the bishop welcomed the prodigal home.

This gradually became an "order of penitents," similar to the "order of catechumens," the major difference being that the penitents had already been baptized once-for-all. The only evidence of "private" penance for those who had fallen away was for the dying. But by the sixth century, few entered the order of penitents voluntarily, and those who did found it an expression of commitment very like the one made by vowed religious today. But in some places, many people became ceremonial penitents for the season of Lent, which corresponded to the catechumen's final preparation for baptism at Easter. By the tenth century, all Christians were expected to be penitents for Lent.

Medieval

From the sixth to the ninth centuries, public penance was gradually replaced by the "tariff" penitential form made popular by Irish monks re-evangelizing Europe after the invasions. They used the unfortunate metaphor that sin left a contaminating "stain" on the soul and the sinner in deep "debt." It was the beginning of a withdrawal from confession with a "Church" dimension to a focus almost entirely on the individual "debtor, paying his debt to God"; each wickedness was listed in a book for priests with a proportionate penance for each (like obligatory sentencing). That insidious economic metaphor again, which ultimately degraded into the literal sale-for-money of indulgences to remit the guilt of past sins, an obscenity that led to the Church being split in half against itself yet again in the Reformation.

While the earliest years had emphasized a second conversion as the price of re-entry into the Church, the middle ages saw "satisfaction" and "making amends" as the cause of divine forgiveness. The metaphor was not "familial" but "economic."

Throughout the middle centuries, theologians disputed back and forth what was required for genuine redemption in the sacrament of penance. Some (Abelard, Lombard) argued that confession and absolution were the outward physical signs of an inward conversion of soul; sinners are forgiven even before they confess, and the function of the priest is to declare definitively that they are demonstrably forgiven. Others (Scotus) believed the confessed sins were not the causes of forgiveness but the conditions for the absolution to be effective. And by the Council of Trent in the sixteenth century (which was unaware of the historical development of the sacrament), penance was even more tightly constricted to a "judicial forum," with the priest as judge, in which the penitent had to bring forward every single sin and tell how many times he or she had committed each—in complete defiance of the penitential practice of Jesus.

Vatican II

Vatican II instituted three different rites of penance: first, the one we're all familiar with, one-on-one; the second, a public rite for many penitents ending in individual confession and absolution;

third, a public rite for many penitents confessing their general sinfulness and receiving general absolution without individual confession. The focus is clearly on the gratuitous mercy of God, on love undeserved but always at the ready, and on the fulfillment of the human soul.

> In the depths of our consciences, we detect a law
> which we do not impose on ourselves, but which
> holds us to obedience. Always summoning us to
> love God and avoid evil, the voice of conscience
> can when necessary speak to our hearts more
> specifically: do this, shun that. For we have in
> our hearts a law written by God. To obey it is the
> very dignity of humanity; according to it we will
> be judged.
> *The Church Today* (16)

The theme of reconciliation runs through all the sacraments, primarily because the truth that undergirds all Christianity is death and rebirth, disruption and starting over again, conversion: individuals want a richer life than paganism can offer, and those on the Ship of Peter reach out into the chaotic waters and "pull them in."

The prime model for the sacrament of forgiveness is the story of the prodigal son. God, like the father in the story, is always forgiving, but the boy had to come home in order for the forgiveness to take effect. The problem in the story is the elder son who, to the end, is still unwilling: better to sulk in hell than serve in heaven. God always forgives; the problem is with the self-righteous—and even more, the indifferent—who feel they have no need of it. Dr. Monika Hellwig makes it very clear:

> What this means is that the repentance and the
> forgiveness are two different ways of describing

the same event. It is not really that the repentance comes first and after that God forgives. It
would be closer to the truth to say the forgiveness
comes first and that is what makes the repentance
possible in the first place.

As with all religion, confession is a "connection" between two
vulnerable persons.

Reconciliation / Spiritual Direction / Therapy

The model for all three—sacramental reconciliation, spiritual
direction, and therapy—is the same: a one-on-one encounter, in
which each person places confidence in the other; all three
encounters are attempts, with wisdom, compassion, and tough
love, to heal alienation—from others, from the world, from oneself.

Penance, given the constraints of time, ought to be a relatively brief encounter; the purpose is forgiveness. But the
confessor should be wise enough to realize when the person's
problem really needs more time and perhaps continuous discussion; then he can recommend that the penitent find someone—a
friend, a relative, a religious, a priest—with whom he or she can
work out the problem of healing on a longer-term basis. But the
confessor ought also to be wise—and humble—enough to
discern when the penitent has a problem so deep-seated that it
can never be healed even by the wisest and best-intentioned non-
professional; then he can recommend that the penitent consult a
good psychiatrist, psychologist, marriage counselor.

But the functions of penance and spiritual direction on the
one hand are quite different from the functions of psychotherapy
on the other. The therapist would never intrude her or

his religious beliefs (or disbelief) on the interchange, nor would they be swayed by the client's religious beliefs (unless they were part of the problem). The therapist is trying to help the client understand what events and relationships in the past have left him or her unable to cope with the present. She wants to lead patients to an understanding, acceptance, and peace with the *causes* of an unsatisfactory relationship with self and others.

On the contrary, the good confessor very much wants to share his vision of human weakness and dignity with penitents; he is after all a forgiven sinner himself. Like the psychiatrist, he wants to begin healing rifts in that "horizontal" moral web of human relationships, but unlike the psychiatrist, he wants to begin healing the "vertical" relationship with God as well. He wants to help penitents understand, accept, and be at peace with the fact that—no matter what the causes—there is a *reason* to feel completely free of the burdens those actions have put on their souls, to *accept being accepted* by God, no matter what they have done. They're "home." At least for awhile, cosmos has replaced chaos once again.

"Spiritual direction" might be too manipulative and regulatory a term. Rather, those concerned with healing or enriching the life of the soul—precisely what separates us from animals and robots—are greatly helped by seeking out someone they know who is *wise* and with whom they can periodically discuss what's going on in their lives, good and bad, with complete frankness. If the person drinks too much, swears too much, loses patience too much, there is no reason to cover it up, especially from themselves. The purpose is to see things—and oneself—*as they are* and to discern together realistic ways of growing more profoundly human and more deeply Christian.

Ambassadors of Christ

The word "mercy" is not really a good translation for the Hebrew *hesed*. It has more the sense of Yahweh's *faithfulness* to Israel despite her constant betrayals. "The mountains and hills may crumble, but my love for you will never end; I will keep forever my promise of peace" (Isaiah 54:10). Nor is God's forgiveness merely a gift simply given and received. It is an empowerment to forgive, as well. The capacity for forgiveness usually arises out of the experience of being forgiven—love undeserved. Jesus invites us to the same: "Be merciful just as your Father is merciful" (Luke 6:36). Jesus healed people despite the Sabbath and despite their being foreigners. In the Lord's Prayer we acknowledge that we will be forgiven only insofar as we forgive. Forgiveness is, in fact, the sole reason Jesus came: to declare the Amnesty of God (Luke 4:19); "This is my blood, which seals God's covenant, my blood poured out for many for the forgiveness of sins" (Matthew 26:28). St. Paul continues:

> All this is done by God, who through Christ changed us from enemies into God's friends and gave us the task of making others God's friends also. Our message is that God was making all human beings God's friends through Christ. . . . Here we are, then, speaking for Christ, as though God were appealing through us.
>
> (From 2 Corinthians 5:18–20)

Jesus said, "This is a cup of my blood . . . so that sins may be forgiven. Do this in memory of me." Not just share the cup but also forgive sins. As learning to cope with the pain of menstruation makes most women more compassionate than most men, so periodic confession makes people less judgmental, more merciful, clear-eyed enough to acknowledge the sin but aware of the weaknesses in their own lives. A father, for instance, whose daughter shocks him with the news she is pregnant and unmarried has several options. He can rant and rave and perhaps beat her; shake a finger and say, "Now this is what you're going to do, young lady"; collapse into self-pity and wonder what he and the girl's mother had done wrong; or put his arms around her and share her sorrow. That last choice is not an act of an in-charge parent; it is an act of love. At least for the moment, the girl's shame is more important than his own shame.

As the theologian Karl Rahner, S.J., wrote:

> Everything depends on lay people's under-standing that they are, as individuals, irreplaceable, with a specifically Christian and moral task to be performed within groups not directly subject to the Church's official control, a task of which they will have to give an account before the judgment seat of God.

> The worst human beings can do to Christ is not to spit in his face, mock him, scourge him, boot him through the streets, crucify him. The worst they can do is ignore him.

Chapter Ten

— ❦ ·•· ❦ —

HEALING: SICKNESS AND DEATH

Happy are those who mourn; God will comfort them!

(Matthew 5:4)

A Puzzlement

He had an improbable name: Bill Fold. A merchant seaman without family, in a terminal cancer ward. His larynx had been removed, and he could communicate only in writing. More debilitating, he had also contracted tuberculosis, so he was in complete isolation; all visitors entering his room had to be gowned and masked.

One day the priest who visited him every week asked if there was anything he could do for him, and Bill quickly wrote on his pad, "I'd like to have the last rites." The priest puzzled. Doctors said Bill could last another year, and at the time, anointing was restricted to those in imminent danger of dying. But the large dark eyes were so pleading that the priest threw caution and Canon Law to the winds, heard Bill's confession, anointed him, and gave him communion.

When it was over, his eyes puddled with tears, Bill wrote on his pad, "I'm so grateful. Is there anything *I* can do for *you?*" The priest thought a moment and then said, "When you get there, Bill, mention my name." And Bill wrote, "I shall."

As he was leaving, the priest said, "Bill, it must get very lonely." And Bill wrote, "Yes. But isn't it wonderful God trusts me enough to give it to me?"

And that night Bill Fold died.

Suffering

Since the rise of the omnipresent electronic media and their total domination of a great part of our lives, we have become thick-skinned to the assaults of others' sufferings on our souls. The anguished eyes of starving African children, raped and battered women, mothers grieving for children shot by strangers are too much to bear. Seeing a drunk or an addict sprawled senseless on the sidewalk makes us avert our eyes as we would from an animal smashed on the road. When students see upperclassmen degrading a freshman, they turn away like the priest and the levite from the beaten man the Samaritan finally rescued. But being so protective of our sensibilities—and our children's, we impoverish our souls.

Every philosopher from Buddha to Karl Marx began with human suffering; if you haven't started there, you haven't started. Any religion asks that fundamental question: Does life have some focal meaning *despite* this suffering I endure? Is there some cosmos in the midst of this disorienting chaos? If God is *both* all-powerful *and* all-loving, then *why* am I visited with this evil? It is the Job question. So too with Christianity; the meaning of suffering is at its very heart.

Whoever wants to follow Jesus to fulfillment is asked to carry a cross (Mark 13:10–13). What is the cross? Being asked to live a human rather than an animal life. Facing suffering not with helpless groans but with dignity. The suffering of Jesus—as with the suffering of Job—is the suffering of the innocent. None of us less wicked than those who perpetrated the Holocaust is deserving of death. Then why would a good God create a world in which the innocent could suffer and all must die?

Some theologians, like Tertullian and Augustine, said that suffering is God's retribution for sin, just as today some very unchristian Christians say AIDS is God's punishment for sexual promiscuity. But suffering, they say, can be offered for others. Such an explanation depends again on the "Economic God."

Who would want to serve a "God" who appreciated the agony of
Job, of Jesus, of children born with *spina bifida?* Pope John Paul
II, in his letter on *The Christian Meaning of Suffering* in 1989,
said that through suffering a woman or man is destined to *go
beyond* the self. Suffering, then, is the doorway to transcendence.
The answer to the question of human suffering is right there: in
Jesus, the Christ.

In the gospels, Jesus never asks any suffering person to "offer
up" that suffering to God, in atonement for their sins or for
someone else's. The God he serves doesn't "require" suffering, but
God does offer suffering as an "opportunity." For what? Why
does God force us from the womb? Why does God force us,
because of our bodies, to become independent of the slavish
attention of our parents? Why does God suggest to our parents
that it's time for us to leave the nest and get shoved into a school?
Why does God set things up so that our childhood innocence
and carefree ease are shattered by the eruption of adolescence?
Why does God—just at the time when we've finally achieved a
measure of independence from our parents—suddenly instill in
us the urge *not* to be alone, but to surrender our newfound independence to someone else in a relationship of intimacy and
partnership? Why does God, once we've established a stable relationship with another human being, set for life, instill in us the
irrational urge to become parents?

Only when you've answered those questions, will you be able
to answer the question: Why does God ask us to suffer and then
die? It's all a pattern, you see.

Just as guilt can become meaningful only when we turn it
into responsibility, suffering can become meaningful only
when—like any other natural crisis in life—it can open our
minds and hearts to wider horizons.

Sister Thea Bowman, dying of cancer, said:

> Perhaps it's an incentive for struggling human beings to reach out to one another, to help one another, to love one another, to be blessed and strengthened and humanized in the process. Perhaps it's an incentive to see Christ in our world and to view the work of Christ and feel the suffering of Christ.

Sickness and the Whole Self

The preamble to the charter of the World Health Organization defines a holistic view of health: "Health is a state of complete physical, mental, and social well-being and not merely the absence of disease or infirmity." The root meaning of the word "health" is completeness, wholeness. Therefore, health involves the *whole* person: body, mind, and soul. Each of us is not—or was not meant to me—just an uneasy composite of antagonistic functions. We were meant to be a *self,* known, accepted, a person we are more-or-less at "home" being.

Sickness does not attack just the body. It attacks a total human being. The illness—whether acute, chronic, or terminal—forces a person to confront the limitations that bodiliness imposes on our souls: our hopes, our dreams, our desire to be meaningful. It is a crisis of faith, hope, and love.

It is a crisis of faith insofar as it challenges not only our trust in God (the problem of Job) but also our faith in life itself. The future which seemed since childhood to stretch indefinitely forward, has now contracted, often to a predictable number of months. "I am no longer independent. I have to yield myself to others." It is a crisis of hope because it defers our plans or perhaps even makes them totally unrealizable. "I can't even control my own life. I'm not in charge, even of my own destiny." It is a crisis of love, disrupting relationships with friends and family. "How can I be such a burden to them? How can I strain their tolerance like this?" When one's life is threatened, it inevitably smallens one's concerns to the self: my pain, my needs, my heartbreak. It is difficult to love when one becomes self-absorbed, devouring the self.

Sickness is the hardest challenge to the soul, the inner self. Nurses, doctors, and aides in hospitals and nursing homes can tell within a day which patients are self-possessed, optimistic, confident, at "home" within themselves, and which are self-absorbed, alienated, bitter, "lost."

If the illness affects the whole person—not just the body but the soul as well, then the approach to healing must be holistic as well, caring for the *whole* person. A nurse's smile and touch are as important as her medical knowledge and skills. As Jennifer Glen, C.C.V.I., writes:

> True healing consists less in cure than in conver-
> sion. . . . the Christian work of healing
> invokes the power of God made available in Jesus
> Christ to enable the sick and all who participate
> in their sickness to resolve whatever aspects of the
> crisis of hope, faith and love stand in the way of
> their wholehearted commitment to the life of the
> reign of God.

It is not only the patient who is involved in this illness but family and friends, too, and also the doctors, nurses, aides, even the people who mop the floors of the ward. They all need healing, need compassion, need reminding not only of their own mortality but of the web of human relationships that bind them to one another and to each of their patients. Just as they can tell which patients have a hold on their own souls and which are fragmented, the patients can tell which of the health givers are truly that, and which treat patients as biological problems and elderly people as so many troublesome sacks of flesh to be warehoused.

Sickness and Sacrament

A sacrament is an external symbol that physicalizes an internal reality, like faith, hope, love. The sacramental activities concerned with the needs of the sick and the dying are not restricted to "the last rites": anointing, laying on of hands, communion, funeral, burial. It is a process that may go on for years, and the sick person can be a sacrament to those around her, and those around her can be sacraments to her.

Picture yourself as a person in a hospital room, having visitors. You see them come into the room, forcing smiles, cheered because you're no longer alone yet praying they won't stay too long, suffering their kindness, telling the symptoms yet again and again. But the believer feels what all sacraments are meant to make us feel: you're not alone. You're at "home."

Because the sick person is impaired doesn't mean that he or she has ceased to be, in a very true sense, a "minister for others." They are living pleas to other Christians for compassion, Christ suffering: "Whenever you did this for one of the least important of these followers of mine, you did it for me!" (Matthew 25:40). But they also witness by their honest faith, struggling against their illness, willingly accepting the challenge of weakness, dependency, indignity and fear with dignity and hope.

We who live in a pagan society which glorifies youth, health, and attractiveness, which tries to deny human weakness and dependency, *need* that reminder that the physically impaired offer us in order to discern the hollow falsity of the "conventional wisdom" about what's truly important. The suffering bring Gulliver into our Lilliputian lives; they remind us of the precariousness of life—and therefore how precious each of our days is. Those who deny themselves experience of the ill, the elderly, the impaired, because of the discomfort, awkwardness, intrusion on their time, impoverish themselves. They deny themselves wisdom.

In today's culture, when the emphasis has shifted almost totally to the technical, medical aspects of the problem, which often are not only painful but humiliating, the need for the support of the community is even more essential, especially in hospitals and nursing homes. We can be sacraments to them. The whole ministry to the sick is not solely on the shoulders of the ordained priest. The fact that the priest does visit the ill and elderly is praiseworthy, but there are far more lay people in a parish. They can visit people in need of buoying up. Neighbors can visit friends who have "taken leave" of the Church and would never tolerate the presence of a priest, and "soften them up," plow before planting.

Medical personnel are also obviously ministers to the sick, not only ministering to the body but to the soul as well. Their kindness and compassion are as important as their knowledge and medicines. Even a nonbeliever can be a minister in that sense, just as the nonbelieving teacher who enables young people to reason makes them more able to respond to the challenge of humanity and Christianity.

Family and friends can be a great comfort and support, a reminder that—even in the hospital—one is still at "home." The sick person does not face the fear and uncertainty alone. But also the parish is that segment of the Body of Christ with which the sick person has been identified. As St. Paul said, "If one part of the body suffers, all the other parts suffer with it" (1 Corinthians 12:26). Not only should the parish assembled at Mass each Sunday join in the prayers for suffering fellow members when their names are mentioned, but they should make the effort to go and see them. We can minister to them in many ways, baby-sit the children while the mother or father stays with a spouse in the hospital, drop off food, run errands.

As we saw, from the very earliest days of the Church, after the Sunday eucharist, family members took bits of the consecrated biscuit home for relatives too ill to attend. Today, eucharistic ministers do the same, coming to the altar toward the end of Mass to be publicly sent from the community to those who still belong, even though they can't be there. The communion service itself is a kind of small rendering of the Mass: a prayer for forgiveness, a brief reading from scripture, then silence or a sharing of insights into the passage, the Our Father, the communion, and a prayer of thanksgiving.

Anointing the Sick

In the New Testament, when Jesus sent out the Twelve, "they went out and preached that people should turn away from their sins. They drove out many demons, and rubbed olive oil on many sick people and healed them" (Mark 6:12–13). But the classic text regarding this sacrament is in the epistle of James:

> Are any among you sick? They should send for
> the church elders, who will pray for them and

rub olive oil on them in the name of the Lord.
This prayer made in faith will heal the sick; the
Lord will restore them to health, and the sins
they have committed will be forgiven. So then,
confess your sins to one another and pray for one
another, so that you will be healed.

(James 5:14–16)

Until Vatican II, the norm to receive this sacrament used to
be "danger of death." Now it is "seriously impaired by illness or
old age." On the one hand, someone cannot be anointed merely
because he or she is mildly "indisposed"; on the other, anointing
after death is forbidden; the soul is gone; the rite can benefit no
one. But what if a person is still alive but in a coma or deranged?
One wonders if Jesus wouldn't do it, for the family. Just as
baptism is primarily for the family, and not for the infant who is
unaware of what is going on, so too anointing. It is not magic:
slipping a sinner past St. Peter with oil on the brow. But the
family has suffered too; they need healing.

The sacrament has a twofold purpose: first, to bring all the
support and encouragement of the Church to the sufferer, and
second, to help them put this challenge into the perspective of
the death and resurrection of Christ. It promises no miracles.
Rather it is a healing of the soul that separates us from beasts,
healing the bitterness, the fear, the loneliness. The ritual puts this
agonizing event into the context where it does have meaning:
eternity. Although within our this-world cocoons the suffering
appears enormous, in the context of forever it is a labor pain
from which new life will emerge, like a butterfly.

Suffering and illness are not in themselves redemptive. In fact
the pain tends to erode faith rather than build it up. But the pain

can become meaningful, even empowering, if the sufferer realizes that it was up the painful path to Calvary that Jesus found rebirth.

Anointing the forehead, the priest prays: "Through this holy anointing may the Lord in his love and mercy help you with the grace of the Holy Spirit." Anointing the hands: "May the Lord who frees you from sin save you and raise you up. Amen."

At present, the only one empowered to administer the sacrament is a priest or bishop. Some theologians argue for a return to the practice of the earlier Church in which lay persons brought oil blessed by the bishop to anoint the ill and dying. And there is much to be said for that. Priests are becoming fewer; deacons are quite often given charge of the ministries for the sick in a parish; there are far more lay people, and they already do bring communion to the sick and elderly.

However, perhaps the priest himself is more meaningful *to the sick person* than his actions, prayers, or oils, at least in the case of the final anointing when death is imminent. For the person's entire lifetime, the Roman collar has somehow "said" God must have a purpose. Its presence "says" we know Jesus went through all this, too, and not only shows us death is inevitable even for the Best of Us but also shows us how to do it well. Again, perhaps not theologically or historically "correct," but somehow psychologically "right."

Oil is a *seal,* as in "signed and sealed." It says, "This is one of *ours!*" And often, as with anointing kings and prophets, it is a sign of mission: "We are sending you on to give witness to us *there,*" as Bill Fold promised he would for the priest who anointed him. But until then, we are missioning you to be witnesses to us, about what faith, hope, and love really mean. But most importantly it unites the sufferer with Christ, the Messiah, the Anointed One.

Touching is very important in Jesus' mission. A woman suffering from bleeding for many years believed that, if she could only touch the hem of Jesus' garment, she would be cured, and so she was (Matthew 9:21). "All the sick kept pushing their way to him in order to touch him" (Mark 3:10). "Some people brought children to Jesus for him to place his hands on them" (Mark 10:13). "All the people tried to touch him, for power was going out from him and healing them all" (Luke 6:19). A man with a skin disease begged Jesus, if he wanted to, to make him clean. "Jesus reached out and touched him. 'I do want to,' he answered. 'Be clean!'" And so he was (Matthew 8:1–3). Two blind men came to Jesus, and he touched their eyes: "'Let it happen, then, just as you believe,' and their sight was restored" (Matthew 9:29–30). Some people brought a man who could barely see, and Jesus put his fingers into the man's ears and touched the man's tongue and said: "Open up!" (Mark 7:33).

The touch was important, but in each case its effectiveness was in *response* to the victim's faith, just as the effectiveness of forgiveness depends on the sinner's felt need to be forgiven.

Laying hands on the recipient of a sacrament—in baptism, confirmation, reconciliation, orders, anointing—is a direct connection between two human beings. The human body both defines us as particular selves and separates our inward selves from others' inward selves. Touch bridges that gap. The imposition of hands at the anointing reenacts all those saving contacts the person has felt with the Body of Christ through touch.

Unfortunately in our society we are very wary of touch. Rather than a way to bridge the gap between our separated selves, it seems a threat, an intrusion within our defenses, almost a violation of some unwritten law. One only has to see how restrained we are at the greeting of peace.

Death

Death seems the ultimate insult. Strive and strive and strive, like Sisyphus, for this? St. Thomas Aquinas, with stark forthrightness, called the last anointing, *sacramentum exeuntium,* "the sacrament of those on their way out." But death was the ultimate insult for Jesus, too. THE most crucial question of human life is Peggy Lee's: "Is that all there is?"

The Greek word *paschein* from which we get the word "paschal" means "to suffer," in the sense of "bearing" or "enduring" something one can't avoid. Suffering means being acted *upon,* yet not in the sense of being totally "passive," but in being "receptive," as one ought to be in prayer. There is a vast difference between death undergone angrily and helplessly like an animal and death understood and accepted, as Jesus' death was: "Father! In your hands I place my spirit!" In a genuinely Christian death, the dying person is not just a "victim" or a passive spectator; he or she is an active agent in willingly surrendering this life in the hope of another, a process we have seen over and over again in these pages. As Dr. Hellwig writes: "If death must necessarily be a passive experience of being taken over by the inevitable in spite of oneself, then life is after all absurd and freedom just a cruel jest."

Final Anointing and Viaticum

"Viaticum" means literally, "food for the journey." In the Greek and Latin cultures, "viaticum" meant a coin placed in the mouth of the dead person to pay Charon, the ferryman, for the journey across the River Styx into the underworld. In the Christian sacrament, the Host is that coin. But it cannot be administered to someone already dead; the person—the self—has already departed. Christians send off their dying with the gift of Life Himself. The gift is not to "pay" for safe passage; it is a provision for the trip.

In *The Pastoral Care of the Sick,* Viaticum is described as:

> The celebration of the eucharist as . . . food for passage through death to eternal life, the sacrament proper to the dying Christian. It is the completion and crown of the Christian life on this earth, signifying that the Christian follows the Lord to eternal glory and the banquet of the heavenly kingdom (175).

The "last rites" are a renewal of baptism, in which they first entered the death and resurrection of Christ. Now they prepare for the real thing. Many theologians argue strongly that the real sacrament of the dying is viaticum, and the Church agrees insofar as, if there is not time for penance-anointing-viaticum, viaticum should take precedence.

Funeral Rites

Although they are not a sacrament separate from the Mass, the ritual of a Christian funeral ought also to be part of the whole process which began with the first anointing, continued through the supportive community during the person's illness, the final anointing and viaticum, and the death itself. But as with baptism, the final rites given the deceased Christian are at least as much for the grieving friends and relatives, who are also in need of healing.

We genuinely begin to grieve when we openly acknowledge that we have suffered a loss. Sometimes it is simply too huge a loss to encompass. But until we yield to the truth, we live an illusion. Then we simply have to express our feelings, or they corrode within us.

Somehow, we have learned to suppress emotions—especially males. It is somehow "out of place," unacceptable behavior to bare our private pain. So we wall it away within, as if we could smother it to death. But like any truth, it will not go away. Instead, it builds poisonously and warps everything we do. It is perfectly natural to grieve, not only natural but healing.

Finally, we must *choose* to let go. A widow, for instance, might refuse to give away her dead husband's clothes or chair or tools, in a form of denial. But, however painful, it must be done. Life has to go on, no matter how unexpectedly different. The rites for Christian death are the community's attempt to help the bereaved cope with that grief.

The Wake

Like all times when we are surprised into a contemplation of the limits which death places on human life, the custom of having a wake—or "watch"—with the dead body present, either with the coffin open or closed, seems a morbid practice to many. True that it is unwise to bring very small children to a wake, nonetheless it is a very salutary—no matter how trying—experience even for children of age ten or so, and surely it is a growing, humanizing experience for adults. Without a felt sense of death, we live a life deceiving ourselves into believing we have an endless number of days, and not valuing each day as precious.

Far more important, however, is the need of those left behind for compassion and consolation. A wake is no time to provide the distraught family and friends with "all the answers." Their sense of loss is not intellectual. Rather, it is confusion, anger, emptiness, sometimes even a guilty sense of relief that their loved one's suffering is over—as well as their own agony helplessly watching it. The mere physical *presence* of friends and neighbors is sacramental: an embodiment of grace, love unexpected and undeserved. And if it is not too embarrassing or inappropriate, putting your arms around the bereaved and communicating solely by touch says "you're not alone."

On the evening before the funeral, those present in the home or funeral home gather for a rite which in a very real way helps take the sting out of bereavement, sharing the loss. The structure follows the structure of the liturgy of the word at Mass: prayers, a scripture reading, a brief homily, and the Lord's Prayer. The rite concludes: "Blessed are those who have died in the Lord; let them rest from their labors, for their good deeds go with them." Then the minister signs the body's forehead with a cross, recalling the signing that first greeted the deceased at baptism and at confirmation: "May the love of God and the peace of the Lord Jesus Christ bless and console us and gently wipe every tear from our eyes: in the name of the Father, and of the Son, and of the Holy Spirit. Amen."

The Funeral Liturgy

The whole progression of the rites for a Christian death emphasizes hope and consolation by immersing the faithful back into the symbols of Good Friday and Easter Sunday, death leading to rebirth. At the door of the church, the minister welcomes the bereaved family in the name of their brothers and sisters sitting in the church. He blesses the coffin with holy water which recalls baptism into Christ's death and resurrection, and covers the casket with a white cloth, like the white cloth draped over a child at baptism.

The procession passes up the main aisle and places the coffin at the foot of the Easter candle which symbolizes the Easter event, the totem rooted in the earth and pointing toward heaven, burning with life. Although the homily may be partly a tribute to the deceased, its primary purpose is to help those in the pews make sense of death, that without the hope of rebirth death makes no sense at all—nor does suffering, or in fact human living. At the offertory, the priest or deacon passes down to the main aisle and incenses the coffin, the smoke physicalizing our prayers for the deceased rising heavenward. Finally, after communion, when some family member or friend may have given a more personal eulogy of the life and character of the deceased, the priest in the name of the whole assembly and the whole Church commends the deceased on his or her final journey.

Burial

The actual burial is the most difficult stage for those who cared for the one dead. It is a final physical separation, and the prayers emphasize our continued hope that one day we will all be reunited forever. The spirit of the moment is captured in such scripture verses as:

> All I want is to know Christ and to experience the power of his resurrection, to share in his sufferings and become like him in his death, in

the hope that I myself will be raised from death
to life.

(Philippians 3:10–11)

The minister prays with and for those gathered around the
grave, asking for comfort, consolation, strength, trust in God for
them and eternal rest for the dead. Then he says—to both the
living and the dead—"Go in the peace of Christ."

Chapter Eleven

MISSION: HOLY ORDERS

They cannot be ministers of Christ unless they are witnesses and dispensers of a life other than this earthly one. But they cannot be of service to human beings if they remain strangers to the life and conditions of human beings. Their ministry itself by a special title forbids them to be conformed to this world. Yet at the same time this ministry requires that they live in this world among human beings, and that as good shepherds they know their sheep.

—Decree on the Ministry
and Life of Priests (3)

A Puzzlement

In the middle 70s, when Barbara Walters still hosted the *Today* show, a priest was a guest to talk about the recent film, "The Exorcist," in which he had appeared. During a commercial, Ms. Walters leaned over and whispered, "You're obviously an intelligent man. *How* can you be a priest?"

Holy Orders

In classical Latin, the word *ordo* was used to designate certain groups in society, as the senatorial order, the order of scribes, the order of matrons—something like a medieval guild. So in the Church, there were the orders of catechumens, penitents, bishops, priests, and deacons. And although priesthood and marriage are primarily rites of mission, they are also rites of initiation into a whole new way of life. They are both *honor* and *munus,* both "tribute" and "burden."

The New Testament mentions laying on of hands in only four places, some of which may not be sacramental but merely a human gesture signifying that the community entrusted individuals with a particular task. In Acts 6:6, for instance, the disciples in Jerusalem chose seven men to free them of the burden of dispersing funds to the needy; they prayed and laid hands on them. In Acts 13:1–3, the elders laid hands on Paul and Barnabas, sending them on a mission. Neither act seems permanently empowering. But in Acts 14:23, Paul and Barnabas appointed elders in every church community and laid hands on them. And in the two epistles to Timothy, even earlier than Acts, we find reference back to what had quite likely been a rite of ordination. The first letter is primarily about Church administration, and the second is a more personal letter to Timothy, encouraging him to endure the burden of dealing with souls in his care. "Do not neglect the spiritual gift that is in you, which was given to you when the prophets spoke and the elders laid their hands on you" (I Timothy 4:14). "I remind you to keep alive the gift that God gave you when I laid my hands on you. For the Spirit that God has given us does not make us timid; instead his Spirit fills us with power, love, and self-control" (2 Timothy 1:6–7).

Notice "the spiritual gift" was not given by the elders or by Paul but by God *through* the laying on of their hands. We can assume from the reference in each letter to imposing hands on Timothy, and from the fact the last two chapters of 1 Timothy are a broad range of responsibilities in overseeing the apostolate and the community that these are letters to a "bishop."

Note yet again: "gifts" from the Holy Spirit are not empowerments in the sense of immediately infusing some virtue, like plugging into an electric current or putting gas in a car. It is a reminder to the recipients that, whatever they are called upon to do for the Kingdom, they are not alone. However there is one power which is in fact "infused." By the sacrament of orders, the candidate is empowered to *sanctify*.

Minister / Official

There are two somewhat conflicting functions in the ministerial priesthood. First and most important is a spiritual power: to call the risen Christ into bread and wine, to forgive sins, to preach the word of God, to heal, to witness vows. From what we can gather about the earliest churches, that was the service the ordained provided the community. But as the Church grew from isolated communities dotted around the Mediterranean into an institution stretching all over Europe, to preserve unity there had to be a structure. Thus over the centuries priesthood in the Church developed a second function: maintaining order, orthodoxy, and loyalty to the whole complex structure. Thus the priest also became an official in an institution. The two roles of minister ("servant") and official ("manager") conflict insofar as the one calls for empathy, vulnerability, a willingness to *be* used both by Christ and by the people. It is in the Jungian sense a very "feminine" attitude. The other "official" sense is more assertive, decisive, directive—"masculine."

In the beginning, when the Church was still suppressed, the submissive side dominated. The ministers—bishops, priests, deacons and deaconesses—were men and women chosen for their virtue and their willingness to serve the servants of God. Gradually, though, as the Church grew larger and needful of organization, the directive aspect began to dominate in the life of the clergy and people and prevailed for centuries until Vatican II. The clergy emerged as men "set apart," with certain civil privileges the laity did not enjoy. The Church became less and less understood as the Body of Christ in which all parts had a role to play, or even as the People of God. Rather it was a very "clericalized" Church to which the people submitted.

In the earliest centuries of the Church we have no evidence they thought of two categories of Christians, one active, the "Church teaching" (the clergy) and one passive, the "Church taught" (the laity). Unfortunately, that division did happen when Christians began to be not only not persecuted but openly acceptable and finally the official religion of the Empire. In 318,

Constantine appointed all bishops to the post of imperial judges, and the episcopacy began to seem more like a jurisdiction than a sacrament. What's more, both in the Empire and after the barbarian invasions, lesser clerics were most often literate, disciplined, and trained to keep confidences. As a result, bishops and priests became valuable civil servants—*clerici,* "clerks—in a strictly secular way; they began to dress, live, and act in a manner similar to their secular counterparts. They became a kind of elitist "gentry."

Also, most adults were already baptized, and their children were routinely baptized in infancy. Christianity seemed to be simply "passed on," like an ethnic Jewish or Polish or African-American heritage, without any need to appropriate it personally and undergo a personal conversion from the world's values to the Kingdom's values. They "wore" their Christianity as routinely and unreflectively as putting on a yarmulke or a dashiki. As "Church" became nearly coterminous with civil "Society," bishops could no longer have hands-on (literally) contact with people in a large diocese and had to devolve onto assistant priests many of the functions bishops had performed in the earliest churches. They became more involved in Church governance than in worship outside their cathedrals.

Even in the documents of Vatican II, such as the *Decree on the Ministry and Life of Priests,* the words "sheep" and "shepherds" occur a bit too often for some sensibilities. Once again, we risk becoming prisoners of our metaphors. Some priests are "pastors," meaning herdsmen; the bishop carries a shepherd's crook as a sign of his office. But the people in the pews are *not* sheep but human beings, many of whom have better degrees than the pastor. They are able to read and reason, and especially in our pluralist society and unlike the medieval faithful, they have sources of information other than the Church.

Perhaps a bridge between priest as minister and priest as official teacher is a different way of understanding the word "teaching." There are two quite different approaches to that process. One is Horace Mann's: two people sitting on either end of a log, talking. That was also the way of Socrates: posing a question and exploring it together. The other way is more "efficient," insofar as large numbers can be led to a "mastery" of predigested data. The difficulty with that style is that the truth of the data is most often never *internalized;* it is not learning but merely "schooling," endured for awhile till we can get out and play. And because it is not internalized, it lasts only until the final exam, if that long.

Since Vatican II, the style in most parishes (if not in most Catholic schools) has become "teaching" in the sense of "learning together," sharing burdens, acknowledging the richness that the unordained laity have to offer our common venture.

The Priesthood

The priest is a *member* of the Body of Christ, not its head; Christ is its head. "There are different ways of serving but the same Lord." (I Corinthians 12:5) The priesthood is one ministry among many in the Body. The priest stands *within* the Church, not above it.

Then how is the priest's role in the Church different from any other genuine Christian's? His function is to sanctify and to challenge: to proclaim the word of God, to offer himself to be used at worship, to enlist the members of his church to care for the spiritually and materially needy. He is a person-symbol whose purpose is to awaken faith in the community, to body-forth

Christ: "It is no longer I who live," as Paul said, "but it is Christ who lives in me" (Galatians 2:20). His very presence at least ought to be a reminder that reality has a dimension larger than the everyday. His inner motivation is a felt need to serve people in a more intense way than the ordinary baptized Christian is called to serve. It is a conscious identification with the priesthood of Christ.

Presiding at the eucharist does not mean "playing the role" of Jesus, but—as jazz "takes over" the musician—the priest allows Christ to "take him over" and "play him." Christ alone is the source of all priesthood, the true celebrant. Other priests can join in that priesthood only insofar as Christ empowers them.

The priest acts *in persona Christi* and *in persona ecclesiae,* "in the person of Christ, in the person of the Church," whenever he speaks the Word, transforms the bread and wine, forgives sins. At those moments, the power of Christ and the power of the People of God is "focused" into him as if he were a lens.

In a document called *As One Who Serves,* the American bishops compare the priest's role to an orchestra conductor:

> The conductor succeeds when he or she stimu-
> lates the best performance from each player and
> combines their individual efforts into a pattern
> of sound, achieving the vision of the composer.
> The best leader is one who can develop the
> talents of each staff person and coordinate all
> their efforts, so that they best complement each
> other and produce a superior collective effort.
>
> *(46)*

The purpose of any parent or teacher is, ironically, to render themselves unnecessary, so that children and students can go out on their own. So, too, the priest—just as Jesus did—prepares disciples and then sends them out on their own. Neither Jesus nor Paul was a presider. They were persuaders.

Priesthood is one thing; priests are another. Just as baptism does not "bestow" faith, and confirmation does not "bestow" the wisdom of the Spirit, holy orders does not "bestow" intelligence, purity, gentleness, open-mindedness, or a universally appealing personality. Ideally, the sacrament would be a testimony that a man has been tested for a long time and is not entirely lacking in those virtues. As with any sacrament, what is bestowed is the Spirit's challenge to develop those potential virtues and the individual's commitment to try. Just as the Church commits itself at baptism to support the Christian growth of a child, so at ordination it commits itself to support the continued death-and-rebirth of a man's priesthood.

In the Old and New Testaments, God chose individuals to "inspire" to speak in God's name. But he chose *this* individual, sometimes angry, like Jeremiah, sometimes grim but relenting, like Hosea, sometimes as welcoming as a forgiving mother, like Luke. God chooses prophets and priests as an artist chooses brushes, some for the broad strokes, some for the fine lines. It is a wondrous thing about the Church: there are priests who can curse like sailors, to bring the Kingdom to dockworkers; there are priests who write poetry, to bring the Kingdom into drawing-rooms; there are priests who are recovering alcoholics, priests who are nonpracticing homosexuals, priests who are wounded just as those they seek out are wounded. We need them all. As long as their wounds are engrafted into the wounds of Jesus Christ.

There is a piece of advice one crusty old priest gives to students: "If a priest ever bawls you out in confession, say to him, 'Father, I came here to find Jesus Christ. And I didn't.' Then walk away, having reminded the priest of the One he has allowed to use him as a means of grace."

Ideally, as John Oliver Nelson puts it, a priest ought to be a "gracious, unassuming, joyful, completely *honest* and dependable servant of God and common folk." At least he must try. And it is consoling that priests go to confession like the rest of us.

How, then, is a Catholic priest *different* from a cultic priest, an agent of Empire, or even from a Protestant minister?

Jewish priests were of the tribe of Levi, "levites," but by the time of Jesus the high priest had become a political appointment, and the levitical priesthood was an elitist "priestly caste." Jesus demanded that his priests reject the arrogance both of pagan rulers and of the self-righteous pharisees. Unlike the levitical power elite, the Son of God became high priest of the new covenant first by humbling himself to become fully human and then by his humiliating suffering and death (Hebrews 4:12–15).

Jesus showed in a most dramatic and sacramental way what he believed the nature of true priesthood was:

> So he rose from the table, took off his outer garment, and tied a towel around his waist. Then he poured some water into a washbasin and began to wash the disciples' feet and dry them with the towel around his waist. . . . "I, your Lord and Teacher, have just washed your feet. You, then, should wash one another's feet."
>
> *(John 13:4–5, 14)*

To the mind of the Son of God, *that* is what it means to be a priest, to serve, to touch, to teach.

The classical explanation of the priesthood of Christ (and by analogy, of all priests) is given in the Epistle to the Hebrews. The key to Christ's priesthood is that, by the incarnation, the Son of God fused himself with humanity, the lightning rod, the channel connecting the divine energy of God with the human energy in our souls. Since we "are people of flesh and blood, Jesus himself became like [us] and shared [our] human nature" (2:14). "Our High Priest is not one who cannot feel sympathy for our weaknesses. On the contrary, we have a High Priest who was tempted in every way that we are, but did not sin" (4:15). Those profoundly felt ties with humanity are what make Christ the Priest (and all priests) not distant and judgmental but compassionate and faithful. "And so [Jesus] is able, now and always, to save those who come to God through him, because he lives forever to plead with God for them" (7:25).

The model of all priests is Jesus' dealing with his own small group of followers. He taught them, served them, even to the point of getting down on his knees and washing their feet. He was patient with their doubts, their skepticism, their wrong-headed ideas of what is important. He even forgave their desertion. The priesthood of Jesus, then, was in *response* to *their* needs—both the ones they openly brought to him, and the needs they didn't even realize they had.

Many Protestant ministers strive to model themselves on that ideal, and some priests try and fail. But what separates the two forms of serving most dramatically is that priests are celibate.

Celibacy

His disciples said to him, "If this is how it is between a man and his wife, it is better not to marry."

> Jesus answered, "This teaching does not apply
> to everyone, but only to those to whom God has
> given it. For there are different reasons why men
> cannot marry: some, because they were born that
> way; others, because men made them that way;
> and others do not marry for the sake of the
> Kingdom of heaven. Let him who can accept this
> teaching do so."
>
> *(Matthew 19:10–12)*

It's interesting that, immediately after that, people bring children, whom Jesus would never sire, to be blessed. And then immediately after that, the rich young man happens along. He has done everything the Law expects, obeyed all the commandments. "Jesus looked straight at him with love" (Mark 10:21). But the young man wanted more, he wanted "perfection," that is, to have the most human fulfillment of which he was capable. Then Jesus offered him a vocation: "Go and sell all you have and give the money to the poor, and you will have riches in heaven; then come and follow me." This was not the call to the ordinary Christian, the call each of us receives in baptism. It was to something *more*. "When the man heard this, gloom spread over his face, and he went away sad, because he was very rich" (Mark 10:22).

The important thing is Jesus loved the man even if he "only" kept all the commandments! That is enough! What Jesus offered was a vocation to serve in the community in a more intense way: to be an apostle like the Twelve. But the man simply couldn't bring himself to do that. Yet Jesus *still* loved him.

A very well-to-do Jewish agnostic once asked a priest why he was celibate, and the priest answered, "I know that love isn't quantifiable, but my energy is very much quantifiable. I figure that, if I were married, my wife and kids would deserve my *best* loving. But loving three or four or five people that intensely isn't enough for me. So I keep my ability to love 'unfocused,' so that whoever shows up gets the full shot."

Surely a priest has more time, mobility, and freedom from legitimate entanglements in order to serve. Yet how can a celibate empathize with the problems of married people when he's never been married? In the first place, a celibate priest is still a human being, and has himself suffered what most human beings have had to suffer in relationships. He knows what it's like to struggle against selfishness—in himself as well as in others, with people who refuse to change for their own good, with being taken advantage of. And his vow of celibacy does not surrender his sexuality, only the use of it. He has wrestled with the mystery of sex quite possibly more than married people, again in himself but also with many others. And, one supposes, if marital difficulties are a large part of the problems brought to him, he has probably made more effort even than most married people to study and understand marriage. What's more, most marital problems are not problems with sex but problems between people. And the priest is a "people."

One could argue that the priest has never had the chance to share a real body-and-soul relationship, the everyday problems of dealing not only with one another but with children for whom you have ultimate responsibility for 20-plus years. Yet it is those very married people who have in fact suffered and enjoyed that relationship who are coming to an outsider for advice. Having had the experience, they don't seem to have been able to reflect on the experience and understand its implications. People come to a priest for advice not because he is an adept

SACRAMENTS: RITES OF PASSAGE 229

sexual practitioner but because supposedly the Church has sent him off for a very long time to become wise.

In fact, one wonders if it isn't easier for a celibate to understand the problems of intimacy in a marriage better than a married person can understand the loneliness of celibacy. Giving up sex is the "easy" part. Far more difficult is never having someone with whom to share your soul totally, never having a child, battling to keep enthusiastic, fulfilled, and life-giving—without having sex. That same wealthy Jewish agnostic asked that same priest, "Honestly, do you mean to tell me you don't have sex?" And when the priest said he didn't, the man shook his head and said, "Then why are you happier than I am?" And he was.

As George McCauley writes, "It is at least arguable that the basis of people's trust in the priest stems in large part from his celibacy, which is a *sign of his commitment* to them.

One does not need to be black, or homosexual, or female, or male, or crippled, or sick, in order to empathize and understand, perhaps even more objectively. A psychiatrist needn't be mentally ill (one hopes), a cardiologist needn't have suffered his own heart attack. But in order to be a good confessor, one does need to have sinned.

The Rite of Ordination

All three ordination rites—bishop, priest, deacon—begin with the liturgy of the word of the Mass. The candidates are then presented to the bishop, elected by him, and the people signify their consent with their applause. All three rites continue with the litany of the saints, during which the candidates prostrate themselves on the floor, like knights keeping vigil before their dubbing. Then in silence the bishop lays his hands on the heads of each candidate, and all the priests present lay their hands on the heads of priest candidates (all bishops present lay their hands on the heads of bishop candidates)—signifying their brotherhood in this power to sanctify.

After the ordination prayer, deacons and priests are vested; a new bishop is presented a book of the gospels, a ring, a mitre, and his shepherd's staff. The bishop anoints the hands of a new priest with perfumed chrism, and he receives bread on a paten and wine and water in a chalice as the instruments by which he will serve the community.

The most basic symbol of ordination is the laying-on of hands. The bishop alone lays his hands on the deacon, but all priests present impose hands on their new brother priests. Again, the oil *seals* the candidate, as in "signed and sealed." The bishop is *confirming* the ordination. Like the white garment given to newly baptized, the vestments are a dramatic visual symbol of a whole new life. The bread and wine and dishes which the bishop offers to the new priest have been given to him at the offertory *by the people.* Again, the bishop acts *in persona Christi* and *in persona ecclesiae.* It is Christ and the people of his Mystical Body who empower this new priest.

> As he presents the gifts to the new priest, the bishop says: Accept from the holy people of God the gifts to be offered to him. Know what you are doing, and imitate the mystery you celebrate: model your life on the mystery of the Lord's cross.

As he presents the deacon with the book of gospels, the bishop says: "Believe what you read, teach what you believe, and practice what you teach."

The Priesthood of the Laity

> You are the chosen race, the King's priests, the holy nation, God's own people, chosen to proclaim the wonderful acts of God, who called you out of darkness into his own marvelous light.
>
> *(1 Peter 2:9)*

Those words were written not for those who have undergone the rite of ordination but for those who have undergone the ritual washing, anointing, and imposition of hands at baptism.

As we've seen before, we as a Church simply cannot lay all the care of the ill and the dying on the ordained priest. There are many other tasks of Christian service that also cannot be "left at his door," like children out of wedlock. If there is a crisis in priestly vocations, perhaps the Holy Spirit is "speaking" through that lack, telling us that laywomen and men must take up a more active role in the priestly people, and not go on expecting the priest to "take care of everything." There are people in the pews with better degrees than the pastor's, better organized, more savvy about financial matters, roofing, floods, grouting in the school showers. Nor can lay Christian service stop within the parish.

Vatican II's *Decree on the Apostolate of the Laity* says:

> The apostolate of the social milieu, that is, the effort to infuse a Christian spirit into the mentality, customs, laws, and structures of the community in which a person lives, is so much the duty and responsibility of the laity that it can never be properly performed by others. In this area the laity can exercise an apostolate of like toward like. *(13)*

Jesus' concern was not merely for his own. He extended himself to Romans, Arabs, even to the self-righteous pharisees—though they refused to listen. He spoke out against the injustice of burdening others with hardships one didn't share, and he whipped the money changers from the Temple. In fact, his criticisms became so threatening to the establishment that they had him executed.

"Ministry" is, as John Futrell points out, "human services performed in response to the human needs of people." It is not profit-oriented or power-oriented, but rather it offers the self to serve; one cannot be useful if one is unwilling to *be used*. Ministry comes from bonding with others, yielding to their needs, cajoling, outfoxing, luring to a larger life. It is love of God expressed *through* love of the neighbor.

It is not a process in which something is "done to" others, with the minister in a higher position than the one served. Rather it is a process of healing and growth which goes on within the one served, with the minister serving as a facilitator, like a midwife at a birth.

Chapter Twelve

MISSION: MARRIAGE

Husbands, love your wives just as Christ loved the church and gave his life for it. He did this to dedicate the church to God by his word, after making it clean by washing it in water, in order to present the church to himself in all its beauty—pure and faultless, without spot or wrinkle or any other imperfection. Men ought to love their wives just as they love their own bodies. A man who loves his wife loves himself. . . . As the scripture says, "For this reason a man will leave his father and mother and unite with his wife, and the two will become one." There is a deep secret truth revealed in this scripture, which I understand as applying to Christ and the church. But it also applies to you: every husband must love his wife as himself, and every wife must respect her husband.

(Ephesians 5:25–33)

A Puzzlement

In the second act of *The Skin of Our Teeth,* Maggie Antrobus tells her husband, George, who is ready to leave her:

> I didn't marry you because you were perfect, George. I didn't even marry you because I loved you. I married you because you gave me a promise. That promise made up for your faults. And the promise I gave you made up for mine. Two imperfect people got married, and it was that promise that made the marriage. . . . And when our children were growing up, it wasn't our love that protected them—it was that promise.

Intimacy and Partnership

Marriage is probably the easiest sacrament to understand because its motivation is easiest to understand. Unlike baptism, confirmation, and eucharist, it doesn't depend so heavily on a perceived and valued Christian tradition and a faith that something unseen-but-real is actually happening. A wedding—even outside a religious context—is very clearly a change, a rite of passage from independence to partnership. A marriage is the basic human experience of what creative, salvific, redemptive love *means:* you are not alone, you are not meaningless, you and I *are* "home."

The key to successful marriage is a paradox: finding the healthy balance between belonging totally to one another, and yet maintaining a unique individuality that will keep each spouse an interesting person, a continued gift for whom each day each partner is grateful. How do we become a "we" while each one still remains an "I"? How can "I love you" mature into "We love us"?

"And they become one" (Genesis 2:24). How can they be both absorbed in the other and yet each still be an autonomous self? Picture a dogwood tree, white or pink. A canny old gardener painstakingly grafts a branch of the opposite color into the tree. After some years, no one can tell whether the original tree was white or pink. They're one tree, pink and white. That's what happens in a good marriage.

The King James version of Genesis says, "Therefore shall a man leave his father and his mother, and shall cleave to his wife: and they shall be one flesh." The word "cleave" has two contradictory meanings. One is to sever, to part or disunite, just as the gardener had cut a white (or a pink) branch from another dogwood. But the other, opposite meaning of the word "cleave" is to join, to fuse, as the gardener grafted the one branch into the other living tree. And the two became one tree. But neither part changed color. The white stayed white, and the pink stayed pink.

That's what happens at a wedding: a young man and a young woman cut themselves off from their families and years of comfortable habits—with no small sense of loss—and fuse themselves into a single, new reality: a marriage. But without losing a sense of being a unique self. Like every sacrament, this is a rite of passage. But, as with every other sacrament, this is only the focal moment in a very long series of moments leading up to it and preparing for it, and also stretching outward before them into the unfathomable future. These two people have been becoming married for quite some time, and they'll become more and more married every day they live together. Every married couple is a *lot* more married today than on the day they first vowed responsibility for one another for the rest of their lives, no matter what.

Like the engrafted dogwood tree, this is a union, a total gift of the self, and yet—ironically—without losing a sense of still being a unique human being. It is a fusion of life stories, and yet there are still two quite different voices telling it. It is not a bad idea, on the anniversary of a marriage—or at least the five-year anniversaries—to have a renewal of those vows for the family and friends, with whom the couple renews their story. (Note: "couple" is singular.) To remember again, explicitly, the moments of happiness and trial, success and sadness. To pledge again fidelity and commitment. Marriage is a gift only insofar as it is a challenge, accepted again and again.

Some dewy-eyed romantics say a marriage is not 50 percent-50 percent but 100-percent gift from both sides. That's far too simple and naive. Even in a fusion as intimate as a marriage, you have to have "a room of your own," a place you can retreat and *be* a self. Otherwise, you become *absorbed* in the other, and by that very fact you have nothing left to give. And part of the paradox of a good marriage is giving the other person the freedom to be an integral part of who-I-am and yet not-me.

If either spouse absorbs the other, the marriage is through. As the poet Rainer Maria Rilke said, the greatest gift two spouses can give one another is "to love the distance between us." You can be pink. I can be white. We're still one tree.

A Rite of Passage

As with all sacraments, marriage is a rite of passage from death to rebirth—death to complete independence, rebirth to a life in which—"no matter what"—you never have to face it alone.

Psychologist Erik Erikson showed there is a purpose to each of the natural crises of human growth, leaving something very good behind for something better. Obviously, birth is a crisis, but without it we die. Weaning and potty training are exasperating to an infant, but without it she would never have any independence. Being shoved out to play is annoying, but without it children would never learn to arbitrate their own disputes without their mommies there. The first day of school is absolutely traumatic, but without it children would never find the skills to get along in society. But the atomic crisis of them all is adolescence.

What the physical changes of adolescence are intended to produce is an *identity:* a personally validated *adult* self, understood and accepted (at least in a broad tentative outline), not just a personality but inner character. That self-possession, in the natural order of things, should prepare one for the intimacy and partnership of marriage. The tragedy is that very few schools try to focus young people's attention on the very purpose of their adolescence. And with so many dysfunctional families, there is little likelihood those children will have any help at home developing character. Thus two people who don't even know their own selves come together and offer those inadequately known selves to one another—forever. Like joining hands with a near stranger and jumping off a cliff. One of the major difficulties many couples have in loving one another is that they've never learned to love—or even know—themselves.

Nor can either one expect the other to make up for what he or she never got around to developing in his or her character during adolescence. She can't "supply" his undeveloped "feminine" side, providing all the empathy, vulnerability, and inclusiveness that he lacks, nor can he "supply" her undeveloped "masculine" side, providing all the decisiveness, determination, and calculation. If they do, the marriage might last, but it is a caricature of two inadequate people: "Oh, the little woman takes care of all that religion business," and, "Oh, my husband does all that checkbook stuff; I have too fluffy a little mind."

One of the best images of a good marriage is the picture of the Chinese Tao: a circle cut in half by a wavy line, one half white, the other half black. But in each half there is a smaller circle of the other color. Stereotypically, the male is decisive, hard-nosed, aggressive, and the female is yielding, inclusive, peacemaking. But she has that small circle within her that demands she also be decisive, hard-nosed, aggressive, and he has within him the need to be yielding, inclusive, peacemaking.

Contract / Covenant

Until the new 1983 *Code of Canon Law,* the word for a marriage was a "contract." Since then, the word "covenant" has been substituted. Paul Palmer, S.J., shows the dramatic difference:

> Contracts deal with things, covenants with people. . . . Contracts are best understood by lawyers, civil and ecclesiastical; covenants are best understood by poets. . . . Contracts are witnessed by people with the state as guarantor; covenants are witnessed by God with God as guarantor. Contracts can be made by children who know the value of a penny; covenants are made only by adults who are mentally, emotionally, and spiritually mature.

When Israel tried to understand its relationship with Yahweh, it looked around for a human counterpart, and the most obvious approximation was marriage. On Sinai, Yahweh took Israel to wife, and no matter how promiscuous Israel became, Yahweh remained ever faithful. The prophet Hosea, in a crazily symbolic gesture, took the prostitute Gomer as his wife, to show how relentlessly faithful God is to his people. Throughout the gospel parables, Jesus pictures himself as a bridegroom, and in Revelation heaven is a wedding feast in which the Son of Man takes humankind as his bride. As Edward Schillebeeckx demonstrates, the Old and New Testaments expressed the relationship between God and us with language taken *from* an understanding of ideal marriage, then turn around and help us understand ideal marriage from God's ideal love of us.

In a carefully worded contract, everybody knows exactly what is involved. But a covenant is open-ended, a total commitment of self to the other, a pledge of personal loyalty, no matter what. Which makes it obvious that couples who draw up "premarital agreements" about who gets what in case of a breakup have—by that very fact—invalidated their vows.

A contract is always bilateral and conditional: I'll do this if you'll do that, and if you don't, you've violated the agreement and I'm released from my obligations. A covenant says: I am *with* you, regardless. No ifs, or buts, or conditions. There's only one rule: We can work it out.

If Christian marriage is an image of the covenant of Yahweh with Israel and the covenant of Christ with his Body, then the marriage must be the same commitment to love without end which Yahweh felt for Israel and Christ feels for his Body. Self-sacrificial love, embodied in the crucifix, is the touchstone of Christian identity and therefore of Christian marriage.

A Sacrament

A very delicate and often painful situation arises when the person exploring married life with the couple about to be married has strong doubts about their genuine eucharistic involvement with the Catholic Church, that this is not a religious commitment but instead that they want a "Church" marriage more for the externals like the music and the dress-up rather than making a genuine religious commitment to one another, calling the People of God to witness it. Quite often, too, the Catholic party is requesting because his or her parents are still practicing Catholics and they want to pacify them. In his apostolic exhortation, *On the Family*, Pope John Paul II acknowledged the couple's natural right to marry, but established norms to determine whether there was faith minimal enough to justify a Church wedding.

As we saw, the word "religion" comes from Latin roots which mean "to bind strongly." Thus, without a serious *connection* to the Catholic eucharistic community, there is no religion, thus no Catholicism. Just as you may be human but not act humanly, you may be Catholic, but you're not acting Catholic.

When a couple asks a priest to preside at their vows, the first question he ought to ask is whether they practice their faith. It needn't be an unbroken chain, but do they at least "come home" fairly often? When they say they don't practice at all, some priests ask each separately to write them a letter saying honestly why they want a priest at their marriage—not this priest as their friend, but any priest, even a stranger, even if their parents aren't going to be there. The letters are quite honest. Sometimes, they result in one or both of the partners seriously reassessing their laxity in religious practice for the first time since high school or college—as adults.

All too often, though, their letters—quite sincere and on the surface seemingly Christian (if not exactly "Catholic")—reveal a "Christianity" which is more tinged with memories of a Catholic childhood than with a present relationship with God and which is, beneath the surface, little more than a genuine, profound, and laudable-if-limited ethical humanism.

One prospective groom wrote that no one could live in any big city without being aware of Christ in agony—the homeless, the disenfranchised, the dead-ended. A moving letter. Though the young man did not attend Mass and, in fact, deferred to his future wife to bring up the children as Jews ("more for ethnic and family reasons than religious ones"), the priest asked if the man himself at least prayed occasionally, tried to sustain a connection to God. He said, "Not really." Yet he still sincerely maintained he was in a very real sense a "practicing Christian" and at least radically Catholic. He was using those words in the same blithely self-deceptive way characters on soaps use the words "making love," when love hasn't the slightest thing to do with the relationship. It was impossible to convince him being Catholic—or even Christian—means more than being just a good human being.

Becoming Married

As we have seen, the wedding is only one climactic moment in a long process of *becoming* married. That process began when the couple began dating, getting gradually to know one another, easy with one another, friendly, testing to find out if this person just might be Mister or Miss Right. When the relationship begins to become exclusive, the couple reaches another stage into a deeper commitment to one another, which can be very precarious when the feelings are overpowering and the commitment is not— because of schooling, finances, unreadiness to take lifelong responsibility for another human being, when one has yet to take full responsibility for her or his self.

When the two finally make a resolve to become engaged and make their intention to commit to one another public, the commitment deepens further, and as in all love relationships the more one invests in the other, the more painful betrayal can be. That doesn't mean that betrayal, that "little death," cannot be turned into a rebirth (just as after the wedding). If the couple can get through those trials—and still love one another—the "little death" has only made the love stronger. Scar tissue is toughest.

The wedding itself is a death to the old and a rebirth as a new composite self, and it can be wrenching. In the Steve Martin remake of *Father of the Bride,* on the night before the wedding, he spots his daughter shooting baskets in the driveway, and she says:

> "I just kept thinking about how this is my last night in my bed and like my last night as a kid. I mean, I've lived here since I was five—and I feel like I'm supposed to turn in my key tomorrow. It was so strange packing up my room. I couldn't throw anything away, so I have all these yearbooks and ratty stuffed animals, my old retainer, all my old magic tricks. I mean, I know I can't stay, but I don't want to leave.

But the comfortable, well-known objects and habits two people surrender to get married are "necessary losses."

The Wedding

Just as the media and advertisers have taken over Christmas, the wedding industries (florists, photographers, musicians, limousine services, caterers) have taken over marriage—or at least the focal symbols in marriage. The couple has to "register" patterns for dishware and silver so friends can give them as presents. Picking gowns for the bride and bridesmaids (never worn again) occupies weeks. The morning of the wedding itself is frequently chaotic (vs. cosmos): one of the bridesmaids has the wrong shoes; the florist forgot Baby's Breath in the bouquets; the white runner down the main aisle snags and looks wrinkled; a huge spray of gladioli on the front of the altar screens off the priest; the country-club reception just about impoverishes the bride's family. Another triumph for the trivial. A woman and a man are pledging their lives to one another, a moment "terrible as an army with banners" (Song of Songs 6:10, *The Jerusalem Bible),* yet a great many of the people present are fretting over stuffed cream puffs and the proper drapery of the bridal train.

Still, a formal church wedding makes it easier for the parents of the couple to "let go," to realize—however painfully, that a new era has begun, a new "little church" is forming. And it involves the whole family and their friends, a community sharing a momentous event and approving it.

Whether the wedding takes place within a Mass or outside, the ceremony is remarkably chaste and simple. After the homily, the priest or deacon asks the couple if they have come "freely and without reservations to give yourselves to each other in marriage." Then they join their right hands and, either in response to the celebrant's questions or repeating the formula after him, they pronounce their vows and exchange the wedding rings the priest has blessed. And it's done.

Despite all the hoopla and folderol which clutter up so many modern weddings, the symbols of marriage are quite simple, too.

Now many priests come down off the altar and stand *between* the couple and the people to emphasize that it is the couple who are the primary ministers of the sacrament, bestowing it on one another and receiving it. And it is the *Church* who ratifies their vows. The priest is merely a lens through which the vows are offered to the people and through whom the people express their approval, and the priest often asks them to symbolize their approval by their hearty applause. At a wedding, no one is merely a spectator.

What do rings "say"? A senior ring, a bishop's ring, Frodo's ring of power? Rings bespeak both constriction and empowerment. Before this moment each was free to choose from all the single members of their opposite sex. But that freedom could not activate until *expended* on the one person, rejecting all the rest. And a ring is a reminder that one is never free of responsibility for the other. But also a reminder that one is never alone.

To stress it yet again: in the Christian myth, "gift, power, honor" are not bestowals but challenges. Grace doesn't "happen" without our rising to the challenge. Jesus constantly told his power-hungry disciples that the true leader is one who *serves* (Luke 22:26). A husband has "power" over his wife only insofar as he serves her; a wife has "power" over her husband only insofar as she serves him. Yet very often true service says, "Thus far, and no further." Marital love *is* loving your "neighbor"—your spouse —with as much tough love as you love yourself.

"Take this ring as a sign of my love and fidelity." Most people seem to think that is restricted to sexual fidelity, and only in the negative "thou shalt not." On the contrary, it is also a pledge of faithfulness to the other's entire being: to stay with you, to forgive you, to understand you—no matter what. As Maggie Antrobus said, it wasn't their love that made their marriage but the marriage promise that made the love possible. Not a feeling. An act of will that takes over when the feelings fail.

The Early Years

Herbert Anderson and Robert Fite call the period of adjustment after the wedding "When the Ordinary Gets Complicated." No problem if both like rock music, but if he loves to play the bagpipes, she ought to know long before they buy an engagement ring. What happens if he's messy, and she's a neatness freak? If he's always ten minutes early, and she's always ten minutes late? Whose family do we have Christmas dinner with? Do we eat liver? Do we smoke? And a very tough one: who holds the remote control for the TV? Do we insert the toilet roll overshot or undershot? "Well, my *mother* always used to. . . ." Especially when conflicting habits are weighed down with family loyalty, it can become like two little kids arguing about who insulted whose mother. None of those little spats is about a genuine "fault," but it is a *difference,* and in communicating and compromising, "we can work it out."

Of the sexual relationship in marriage, little need be said except that it is now a sacramental relationship, physicalizing grace to one another, every time:

> A man should fulfill his duty as a husband, and a woman should fulfill her duty as a wife, and each should satisfy the other's needs. A wife is not the master of her own body, but her husband is; in the same way a husband is not the master of his own body, but his wife is.
>
> *(1 Corinthians 7:3–4)*

It's based on the simple theological fact that God *made* sex, and therefore it's unassailably *good.*

Which might provide an occasion to speak of premarital sex. The ideal honeymoon is delirious, and it lasts longer than just the week or two during which the couple goes off by themselves. In most cases the relationship is highly sexual, intoxicating, out-of-this-world, and it is often the sex that puts all the little spats into perspective. But if the couple has had a serious sexual involvement for a couple of years before the marriage, they've already had their honeymoon. That is the tragic result of living in a society that takes a reality so wondrous and precious as sex and making it commonplace.

The words "trial marriage" are an oxymoron, a two-word contradiction. You can't "try out" a lifelong promise.

Nor is the intimacy in marriage merely sexual. This is not merely a union of two bodies but of two entire selves, body, mind, and soul. Far more important is deepening their *emotional, spiritual* intimacy which many males confuse with sexual intimacy. Emotional, spiritual intimacy involves being willing to be *vulnerable,* not just physically but with the whole *self,* which, ironically, takes a great deal of inner self-confidence. It means letting the hair down, letting the other wander around those dark caverns in the soul. Which in turn takes both courage based on one's own lovability and faith based on the love one is certain the other has for him or her. Oddly, such emotional honesty is a burden two share, which bonds them more closely. Being understood and accepted is more important than being right—or perfect.

The couple has to have the freedom to be a self but also the inner freedom to *reveal* that self. Even after that free commitment in a marriage rite, the couple can still remain unfree, hiding their true selves from one another as Eros hid himself from Psyche, coming to her only at night, an adolescent sexual relationship waiting for hardships to rebirth it into love. Like the fallen Adam and Eve, the couple hide their "nakedness" with fig leaves because they themselves are uncomfortable with who they are. That is why the sacrament of marriage is—or can be—a continual redemption from enslavement to self-doubt, self-distaste, self-deception. Freely and unashamedly, I have allowed someone else to come into my innermost self, to walk around and see all the scars, the ghouls and demons, the fears and weaknesses. And he or she says, "So what? You're still mine. I'm still yours."

As the early years progress, the intoxication of romance slowly neuters down because of the intrusions of reality. Then the couple can begin to learn the difference between being-in-love and loving. There aren't many real love songs. The only one that comes to mind is "Do You Love Me" from *Fiddler on the Roof,* when after 25 years of a prearranged marriage, Tevye asks his wife Golde if she loves him. All that time, they've just been too busy even to think about it. And she answers:

> For twenty-five years I've lived with him,
> Fought with him, starved with him.
> Twenty-five years my bed is his.
> If that's not love, what is?

All the other songs are romantic songs, being-in-love songs: "You are the promised touch of springtime; I can't live without you; you're my everything." Romance is a wonderful, exhilarating, transforming feeling. But it is only a feeling. Genuine love has nothing to do with palpitations of the heart and heavy breathing. Real love is an act of the will; it takes over when the feelings fail, when the beloved is no longer even *likable.* Genuine love is very undramatic, sharing the very down-to-earth chores: living within a budget, putting out the garbage, getting up to change the baby in the middle of the night. Not poetry, just prose: providing, encouraging, giving pleasure, conversing, planning—and giving us the grace to laugh at ourselves.

The process of the first years of becoming married is *bonding*, facing not only the challenges of intimacy but the challenges of partnership. The bonds that web their relationship form in all kinds of small ways: going to a garage sale, refinishing furniture, doing the dishes, making love, visiting one another's families, buying Christmas presents, trying to balance the checkbook together, going to church. Many mature couples want to postpone marriage until they are both very well established in their careers and have a nice tidy sum in the bank. But older couples say the struggles to make it in the early years, together, was the solid foundation of their later life.

Part of becoming well married is letting go of unrealistic expectations, of living not with an idealized Cinderella or Prince Charming but with a flawed-but-loved human being. Still, it is also a commitment to keep one another growing, which means change, "little death" and rebirth. It means creating a climate of acceptability in which, if she wants to go back and get her degree, he'll find some way to empower it, and if he wants to take a year off and write his novel, she'll find a way to support him. That doesn't happen when a couple watch TV every night.

In an ever-growing marriage, a husband or wife ought to be able to say as St. Paul says to the Philippians, "I thank my God every time I remember you" (1:3).

Ecumenical Marriages

If two spouses come from different religious traditions—and each is important to them, or if one has a radical intolerance for religion while it is important to the other, and they simply go ahead thinking "things will work themselves out," they have very unrealistic ideas about what married love can accommodate.

In the view of the 1917 *Code of Canon Law,* the marriage partners were either Catholic or not. The non-Catholic either signed a form which said he or she promised to raise the children Catholic, or a Catholic marriage couldn't take place. But in 1967, Pope Paul VI removed that barrier and said that only the Catholic party in a mixed marriage signs a form which says:

> I reaffirm my faith in Jesus Christ and, with God's help, intend to continue living that faith in the Catholic Church. I promise to do all in my power to share the faith I have received with our children by having them baptized and reared as Catholics.

The non-Catholic needs to be aware of that promise, but is not bound by it. Before the marriage, the couple should be aware that all future decisions must be made jointly, and their capacity to make a good marriage commitment should really be a norm of whether they can honestly enter into a marriage commitment. If one or other has a serious conscience problem on that point, it is a clear indication that they ought to rethink.

Some parents dodge the problem and tell themselves they will let the children decide for themselves when they grow old enough to choose. But, first, when does that age come? And, second, how will children even come to realize that a relationship with God is important, if their parents fob off the responsibility on them? And, third, how will they decide among all the religions which one to choose? And if it becomes a matter of choosing between the father's religion or the mother's religion, it becomes an agonizing choice between the mother and the father.

But truly ecumenical marriages can be a marvelous experience, not only for the couple but for their families and for all the people present for the marriage—and for the ministers themselves, to realize that we are all Christians, or that at least we are all believers in a dimension larger than the merely earthly. If the marriage takes place in a Catholic church, the Catholic priest is the "minister of record," receiving the vows and signing the certificate; if in a non-Catholic church, the priest can take an active part (reading, homilizing, giving the nuptial blessing), but the non-Catholic minister or rabbi receives the vows.

Canon 844 of the 1983 *Code of Canon Law* allows a Catholic minister to permit other Christians to share in the eucharist, reconciliation, and the anointing of the sick (a) if they spontaneously request the sacraments, (b) are unable to receive them from their own minister, (c) are aware of what they are doing. The sacraments are not meant to "lure" a member of one Christian sect into another. Canon 1183 of the new Code allows Catholic priests or deacons to officiate at funerals of other Christians if that was evidently the will of the deceased or if the proper minister of the deceased is unavailable.

That, surely, is not the last word on the sacrament of marriage. But perhaps the last word of all regarding Christianity and Catholicism and marriage is one word: forgive.

Epilogue

SOME METHODS OF PRAYING

Preparing

No runner gets onto a track, no soccer player goes onto a pitch, no actor or dancer makes an entrance on a stage without warming up. They are not only limbering up their bodies and voices but psyching themselves out of one life into a completely different one. So too with praying. Anyone wanting to pray should follow the same preparation exercises, no matter what method of praying proves most conducive to the individual.

- Time. Make an interior commitment of the next ten or fifteen minutes or half-hour. It's set aside from the everyday into the sacred. At least for that time, the world can get along without you. And have *no expectations!* You're letting God do the work. Perhaps all that will happen is that you experience peace. Isn't that enough? Perhaps you have the exhilarating sense of not being alone, of being in another Presence. Isn't that enough? Expect no lights or revelations.

- Place. This will depend on the individual. Some find a church or chapel best; others prefer sitting in a park; some like walking. The main thing is to find a place with the fewest distractions to break the "connection."

- Position. If you are staying in one place, the configuration of the body is important. If you sprawl, you'll fall asleep for sure. Sit on a chair or pillow, back straight, legs crossed Indian-style, your hands opened upright on your knees. You are focused and comfortable, and your whole body "says" receptivity. Most keep out distractions best by closing their eyes.

- Letting Go. It is important—physically and psychologically—to let go, to stop trying to control what happens, to dominate God or manipulate God's will. Roll your head around your neck; many of us can feel the muscles grinding against one another. Let all the tension and concerns drain out of your head into your shoulders. Imagine them as something physical or like waves of energy draining down your back and arms, into your legs and seat, and out into the chair. Now you are ready—not passive, but receptive.

The Mantra

To use a mantra (a constantly repeated phrase), focus your attention on your breathing. Breathe very deeply, in for five counts, hold it, out for five counts. Over and over until you get an easy, steady rhythm.

The most famous mantra is "OM," repeated over and over, feeling the vibrations in one's chest, mouth, arms. I have no idea what it means, if it has any meaning at all, but it works. "The Jesus Prayer" mentioned in Salinger's *Franny and Zooey* is another: on the intake, "Jesus, Son of David," and on the exhale, "Have mercy on me, a sinner." But you could use any words repeated over and over: "Father," "Mother," "Love."

The purpose of a mantra is to short-circuit the calculating intelligence that keeps to schedules, balances budgets, figures things out. It opens up—in males or females—what Jung called our "feminine" dimension: receptive, nurturing, conceiving. The object is to be like Our Lady at the annunciation: "Be it done unto me as you will." To conceive Christ in us.

Many people say they no longer pray the rosary because they can't keep their attention on the words. But the whole *purpose* of the rosary is that you *don't* concentrate on the words, that they set up a rhythm in your mind and soul that goes *beyond* words. It sets up a "being-with," a connection.

Scripture: Mulling Ideas

After preparing yourself, open the scriptures at any place and center the focused inner powers of yourself on what God is trying to say. (Best to start with the New Testament; the Old Testament can provoke too many problems for the beginner.) Make the section small, no more than a few verses. "What are these strange words trying to say to *me?*" Don't probe the words. Let them manipulate *you.* Roll them over in your mind and soul.

If you are unfamiliar or uneasy with scripture, try these:

—Isaiah 6:6–8   —Romans 7:4–6
—Matthew 25:37–40   —1 Corinthians 13:8–13
—Mark 8:31–33   —Ephesians 3:14–19
—Luke 14:12–14   —Philippians 2:5–11
—Luke 1:1–5 9–14   —Hebrews 5:1–4

"And the word of God came to me saying. . . ." What does it *mean?* How to I translate this to the people around me?

Scripture: Controlled Daydreaming

The difference is in mulling over the *ideas* in the scriptures and *reliving* the scriptures. What Jesus said and did "speak" today more movingly than his words or actions.

Relax, let go of the world, read the scripture passage and then in your imagination slip into the scene—as any one of the participants. Earlier we spoke of becoming Jesus at the Last Supper, going from one to the other on our knees, washing their feet—then looking up and seeing the people in our class or office or faculty peopling the table.

Taste the herbs in the food; *smell* the sweat, the dry reeds on the floor, the candle wax; *feel* the textures of the tablecloth and sandals and the benches; *hear* the words not only in your ears but in the stirrings of the hair on the back of your neck; *see* the drab colors, and Jesus etched against that background. Now go through the scene not as an observer but a participant.

We are all no more than matchmakers, trying to make God an appealing friend.

I have done my best. I now withdraw.

REFLECTIONS

Chapter 1

• (Page 8) Reflect on your ordinary week, the constants that give it "shape," the unavoidable requirements you have to fulfill on a regular basis, the duties "others" take for granted that you will fulfill. What are they?

Now imagine waking up one day when the alarm failed to go off. Nobody is around. You begin to suspect there may have been an atomic bomb or something. There's no work to go to, no school, no shopping to do. The electricity is off, and there is no TV or radio to tell you the weather report or the latest news. What would you do? Write it like a short-short story.

• (Page 11) The weekly schedule is very often drudgery, a bore, an irritating intrusion on one's freedom. But what does it do to your psyche? What does it supply that is essential to your sanity?

• (Page 17) Reflect again on your week. What are the times you hold "sacred," not restrictively religious but at the very least non-secular, elements of your life that have nothing to do with the "empirical, this-worldly, secular, pragmatic, contractual, hedonistic, disenchanted"? Are they frequent or rare? What effect do their frequency or rarity have on your psyche, your soul, your self?

• (Page 27) Honestly facing the alternatives—one liberating and the other condemning us to extinction—not many of us have the courage to say, "There is no God." What concrete evidence do you have in your knowledge and experience that convinces you—or at least leads you to suspect—that there is a greater likelihood that there is a God than that there is not, that it is not just wishful thinking to trust that death is only a comma and not a period, that we will go on?

Reflect on the apparent design of the universe, the apparent plan of evolution, the construction of the human body (which no human mind could construct from scratch). Reflect on the undeniable human hungers to find answers and survive death; considering the law of the survival of the fittest, why would those two hungers not have long since died out; and why do the apparently most fulfilled human beings we know of pursue those hungers with an almost fanatical joy? Reflect on the lives of those you know or have read about who truly believe in God, the transcendent, the sacred in life—not merely the half-hearted or the dutiful, but those who believe passionately. Are their lives different from your's? How?

• (Page 33) In the film *Network,* a mad prophet—a former newscaster on the worst network in television and fed to the teeth with the lies and corruption of the network and the advertisers and even of the news—finally goes berserk and tells his viewers: "I want you to go to your windows and throw them up, and stick out your heads, and shout, 'I'm mad as *hell!* And I'm not gonna *take* it any more!'"

All right. You've done that. *Now* what do you do?

Chapter 2

• (Page 41) The purpose of these pages is to offer or at least to underline the existence of that invitation to form a personally validated self—a character, a soul, a self—of that invitation to a larger life than the life available to a dumb animal, an automaton, a personality without substance. The question is whether you as an individual want to accept that invitation.

Probably no reasonable person would say he or she does *not* want a better life than that. Yet the actual decision to set out on the journey requires a *conversion,* a turnabout from one's comfortable former habits. ("Habit is the great deadener.") It means a conscious effort and commitment to read more widely in order to explore greater horizons. It means taking more time out of the rush of the day to reflect.

Ask yourself if you honestly do want to commit yourself to activating the human potential—the soul—within you. The inertia we share with animals doesn't take readily to change and effort. If you draw back from the invitation to live a more fully human life, what are the obstacles that root your resistance? How could they be overcome? Would that be worth it?

• (Page 46) At least begin to evolve a personal answer to the most important and profound (and seldom posed) question: What are people *for?* Or, to put that same question in other forms: What does "success" *really* mean? What does a totally fulfilled human being look like? What must I do, or have, or achieve to be happy?

• (Page 48) The first step toward making peace with the unchangeable is surrendering all the frustrating, self-defeating "if only's." Any statement that comes after those two words is, *ipso facto,* impossible: "If only I were taller, if only I had different parents, if only I hadn't done that."

What "if only's" plague your thoughts at times: the ill-focused resentments about what the world and life and family and work and school have dumped on you? Take some time and list them.

Now, what's the only sensible thing to do with that list—and with all the impossibilities on it?

- (Page 49) Marriages don't just "happen." They take work: reflection, creativity, effort. What is the state of the "marriage" between the "masculine" and "feminine" in your soul? There may be no problem in being genuinely proud of areas where it is quite balanced. But without getting nervous or self-protective about it, how could that balance be improved? What does your soul need in order to be healthier?

Chapter 3

- (Page 61) The human body is a remarkable example of a perfect "society," each of the parts working together for the common good, 24 hours a day: sorting, digesting, storing, trashing, healing. Inside each of our bodies, there is a control center, a message network, a repair crew, a garbage control—all working without any governance from ourselves. And the parts only rarely go on strike if they are mistreated.

What does that organic interaction suggest to us about the way to run our societies?

What does that organic interaction suggest to us about the way to run our souls?

- (Page 70) Recall the most harrowing incident in your life. Not as dramatic as Luke's duel with Darth Vader or Dorothy's encounter with the flying monkeys, but it did wrench your life out of the everyday routine. Describe it with as much detail as you can, especially what was going on *inside* yourself.

Having endured that "little death," that "mini-hell," how was the person—the soul—who emerged from it different?

Chapter 4

• (Page 79) This will take about fifteen minutes; in the
Lilliputian perspective, that may seem a lot of time; it's not.
We're dealing here with the most important thing in your life:
your self, your soul, your meaning. It is the most important
reflection in the book.

First, find a place you can be relatively undisturbed: no
phone, no sirens, no TV, a room where you can shut the door on
the world for a few moments or a secluded part of a park. Sit
quietly, eyes closed. Roll your head around your neck and get rid
of all the tensions, all the obligations, and let them drain down
from your head into your shoulders, into your back, then down
your back into your seat and away. Peace.

Then focus on your breathing, but take really *deep* breaths,
in for five full counts, out for five full counts. Over and over
until you feel a soothing *rhythm*. Then consider your breath.
That air keeps you alive. We have no idea where it's been, but we
use it and pass it on. Ponder that for as long as it "feeds" you.

Then expand your awareness—and your self—beyond the
little circle of peace where you sit, out into the surroundings,
beyond the walls or the trees. In your imagination move
gradually beyond this city, this county, this state, this country.
The air that enlivens us moves eastward across the country, across
the Atlantic, Europe, Asia, the Pacific, and back to us. There you
are, focused, at the center of that enormous enlivening reality.

Finally, realize that the word for breath is *ruah, pneuma,
anima:* spirit.

> Oh, morning, at the brown brink eastward,
>   springs—
> Because the Holy Ghost over the bent

World broods with warm breast and with ah!
    bright wings.
That is your true meaning. That is your true
    "home."

• (Page 82) Job, the perfect and upright man, suffered incredible torment, and he racked his mind trying to find some *reason* to justify it. But his friends insisted he must have done some wickedness, since God does not punish the innocent. Finally, after nearly 50 pages of debate, back and forth, the Lord himself appears in a whirlwind and says: "Where were you when I made the world? If you know so much, tell me about it." It is an overwhelming utterance; read it: Job 38–41. Then try to explain Job's response to it.

I know, Lord, that you are all-powerful;
    that you can do everything you want.
You ask how I dare question your wisdom
    when I am so very ignorant.
I talked about things I did not understand,
    about marvels too great for me to know.
You told me to listen while you spoke
    and to try to answer your questions.
In the past I knew only what others had told me,
    but now I have seen you with my own eyes.
So I am ashamed of all I have said
    and repent in dust and ashes.

    (Job 42:2–6)

• (Page 88) Consider what the poet says about his relationship to God—and God's relationship to him. Does what he says give you any insights in the God-you relationship?

Batter my heart, three personed God; for you
As yet but knock, breathe, shine, and seek to
    mend;
That I may rise and stand, o'erthrow me and
    bend
Your force to break, blow, burn and make me
    new.
I, like an usurped town, to another due,
Labour to admit you, but Oh, to no end;
Reason, your viceroy in me, me should defend,
But is captived and proves weak or untrue.

Yet dearly I love you and would be loved fain,[1]
But am betrothed unto your enemy:
Divorce me, untie or break that knot again,
Take me to you, imprison me, for I
Except you enthrall[2] me, never shall be free,
Nor ever chaste, except you ravish me.
                              —John Donne

• (Page 92) All of us, at least in our more reflective
moments, want to live the one life we have to its fullest. What
are the obstacles (not from outside but from inside)—the idols—
that keep you from complete possession of what Jesus said he had
come to bring—more abundant life? In what ways are you poor,
captive, blind, oppressed—again, not by others, but by self-
imposed enslavements that bar the grace of God?

-----

1. Gladly.
2. Enslave.

Chapter 5

• (Page 102) Look around your room. List all the things you see that have more meaning to you than they would have to the audience at a public auction. Why are they meaningful, "charged"? Then say what each of them—one by one—tells about who the invisible inner "you" is.

• (Page 105) Consider your own participation in the eucharistic ritual at Mass. Does it "work" for you? Many say they stopped going because they "didn't get anything out of it." Is that really the purpose of the Mass? Other than showing gratitude, it surely is, because any sacrament is intended to be a channel of grace, a greater aliveness, the "connection" to God.

Part of the reason might be that the Mass is poorly done—an ill-considered and inconsiderate homily, lackluster music, a graceless "performance." But that is not all of it. You could have a "script" by Shakespeare or Arthur Miller, a priest with all the charisma of Robin Williams, music ministers as talented as a Broadway cast of *Damn Yankees,* but if the members of the congregation are uptight and loath to open up, nothing will happen. No battery can charge anything when the receiver is turned off.

Jesus never worked miracles to provoke faith but only in *response* to it. Is it possible that the failure of the ritual to provoke a felt inner change in you has something to do with you, as well? Any ritual is an attempt to externalize one's beliefs, but one cannot externalize a belief that is hardly there. "Lord, I believe. Help my unbelief!"

• (Page 108) In our dealings with God, through Jesus Christ, each of us stands somewhere along the spectrum stretching between the two extremes: transcendent and immanent, the distant and unapproachable God of the Deists and the intimate gods of the pagans. In your own "connection" with God, is God perhaps too far away and judgmental? Or perhaps too buddy-buddy, a pushover, with very little of the "overwhelming mystery"?

Describe your relationship with God.

• (Page 112) How do you serve as an alive, active member of the Body of Christ?

Think of all the people you come in contact with every week—not just family, friends, next-door neighbors, but plumbers, mechanics, cafeteria workers, secretaries, managers. List them if it helps. Which ones are not living life as abundantly as they could? And how might you at least try to change that? Choose just *one*—and it needn't be the most difficult one.

• (Page 112) Is it possible you sell yourself short, or avoid the challenge, or concentrate on your shortcomings rather than—like Peter walking on the water—keeping your eyes only on Jesus?

• (Page 117) Very honestly, how much "magic" is there in your life? Where does it really manifest itself? If there is little or none, do you feel impoverished? Missing something very important in a fully human life?

What is your sensitivity to the numinous in nature? The symbols of the Church? If there is little or none, is it possible you're missing something?

Chapter 6

- (Page 120) Think of a time when you felt, "I'm absolutely *famished!* I could eat a horse, *raw!*" Those times have probably been relatively rare. There have been times in human history when many people were *that* hungry, when they would eat weeds or worms or roots. There have been times when, as in *Alive,* Catholic soccer players downed in the Andes ate the bodies of their own friends. They considered it a kind of "communion," the dead keeping the living alive.

Why is it that you have never been that hungry? Why is it that you've always had the fridge, a few dollars in your purse or pocket to buy a candy bar or a bottle of soda? What effect has that had on your ability to understand the lives of most of the people with whom we share this planet? What effect has it had on your ability to value the eucharist?

A wise man once said, "Too much is as least as dehumanizing as too little." What does that mean?

- (Page 120) Think about bread. It is so commonplace—like the people we love—that we hardly ever think of it. We pick it off the shelf, toss it in the cart, carry it home, store it, and go for it when we're ready. But trace its history back, even before planting the seed: harrowing the ground, clearing the rocks, breaking the clods of earth. Trace the "history" of the last piece of bread you ate back to its very beginning. How many people have done how many things to that seed before it got to your table? "The product of human hands." Do those words mean anything different to you after that reflection than they did before? If not, why not?

"I'm telling you the truth: a grain of wheat remains no more than a single grain unless it is dropped in the ground and dies" (John 12:24). What does that mean, not to the gospel, but to you?

• (Page 120) Think about wine. Some of us don't have much experience with it, either because we're too young or too strapped for cash. Perhaps our rare experiences of it might make it more valuable than to people who have it all the time.

Like wheat-to-bread, grape-to-wine is a process, even longer than wheat-to-bread. The seed takes far longer; the roots dig down, the vines slowly begin to spread out along the wires, sucking water from the earth and life from the sun. Pruning, weeding, waiting. And waiting.

The wine is the blood of the grape. It must be crushed—that is, die, like the grain of wheat—in order to give the freedom and joy that distilled spirits can give. Just so, the blood on the doorposts of Egypt was the beginning of the Hebrews' freedom, and the blood sprinkled on them in the desert was the sign of their covenant with Yahweh as a new people. And Jesus uses wine as the embodiment of his own blood to mark our freedom and our new covenant with God.

Does any of that have any *felt* meaning for you? If not, can you say why? Is it possible that, without your knowing till now, there is a great deal important about the possibilities of human life that you've been missing out on?

• (Page 123) Set aside for a moment all the irritating surface details about the liturgy and focus on the reality it celebrates: death and rebirth. Does that pattern seem to make more sense out of life than just enduring it: this, and then that, and then the other? Then dying.

Perhaps there is need for a prior meditation: on death itself. Unless death is real to you, the entire meaning of the gospel and the eucharist is empty. It might seem morbid to "wrap your mind around" your own inevitable death, but actually it is quite liberating. Your death is, undeniably, the one event in your future of which you can be absolutely certain. Yet at the same time it is unpredictable; it could be 50 years from now; it could be tomorrow: a drive-by shootist, a drunk driver, a lime tick, a clumsy tackle.

Your death is not only inevitable and unpredictable, but it is also final—at least here on earth. What, and more importantly whom, would you miss? "Owning" your death—and theirs— makes them all the more precious, doesn't it? It's more difficult after that to take them for granted.

What are the grudges that seem so important to you? How do they look compared to the Gulliver of death? Are they worth keeping, or would you be more free if you made peace?

What are the realities you can take with you *through* the doorway of death? Surely none of the realities the media have been selling to you as important since your diaper days. Surely not the bodies so many work on so diligently. Only your self. Your soul. The invisible you no one sees and we can only guess about.

What will you have to take with you when you go?

• (Page 130) Think back to the rather grim first chapter: Gradgrind, Gregor Samsa, Didi and Gogo, the Nazi camps, the enslavements of our own lives. We might not realize the ways in which we ourselves are unfree and contribute to the unfreedom of others. We might be just too busy to notice. For instance, on any given night, you are free to do just about anything: watch TV, go out with friends, read a book, paint a picture, play

Monopoly with the family, do homework, take a walk. But—honestly—to all intents and purposes, if nobody asks you out, aren't you pretty much enslaved to the Tube? How can you be free if you don't assess your options? How can you be free with only one genuine option—which isn't really a choice at all?

Ironically, to be free *costs*. It costs the time to assess one's options, without fear, to settle on a line of action, without fear, and to make a commitment to follow it, without fear. That commitment, of course, closes out all the other options. Freedom is like money in your pocket, nice to know you have it, but of absolutely no value whatever until you expend it on something you want *more* than you want the money, more than you want "keeping your options open."

Is it possible that—without realizing—you do in fact have "the slave mentality," the conviction that "they" are in charge—society, the government, the media, your own moods? That "nobody can do anything about anything," especially not me?

The questions to ask yourself are: Do I genuinely *want* to be free? And am I willing to take the unavoidable steps to lay hold of that freedom? Do I really want to surrender habit, "the great deadener," in order to live life more abundantly, to suffer a "little death" in order to be reborn?

• (Page 134) Like a prior reflection, this one may take some time, but it is absolutely essential. If this is done in a group or with another person, it is worth taking even half an hour, calmly, serenely.

First, list the names of all the people you truly love and who you know truly love you. Don't rush. There may be many more than at first you think. When those names run out, think of the people you really enjoy being with, whether you'd feel at ease putting the word "love" on the relationship or not. Again, don't move on too quickly. Daydream awhile. When you've finally "run out of steam," pause and ponder the truth that one day you will inevitably lose them. Think about that a long while.

Then list all the things in your life you really like: music, books, running, quiet evenings by a river, ice water after a workout, movies. Just keep going until the list peters out. Then mull some more. Then pause and ponder the truth that you might never have known those joys. Think about that a long while.

Finally, if the Giver of all those gifts—which we did nothing to "deserve"—asks, "Do this in memory of me," what would be the only response any person of honor could give? What kind of person would refuse?

• (Page 138) Consider again the moments you reflected on before when you experienced the numinous in nature. That presence was the *anima mundi,* the power of the Artist radiating from what God created.

Consider again the Hindu custom of greeting one another with palms pressed together at the forehead: "The divine in me bows to the divine in you."

In the light of those experiences, consider the moment at which the priest, in the name of the Body of Christ, says the words of consecration, when the Timeless focuses himself from beyond time into the bread and wine—and, through them, into us.

No matter how "boring" the Mass is to the shallow-souled, no matter how routine it *seems,* is that problem perhaps more a problem of sensitivity in those who criticize it?

Chapter 7

• (Page 148) Consider the question posed in this chapter about the radical difference between the attitudes, priorities, and actions of early Christians and their pagan neighbors. They were clearly 180-degrees opposite to one another. But it is also claimed that in the last fifty years, the culture that surrounds us at every turn has become just as pagan as Rome was. If in our day Christianity were once again a punishable offense, what hard evidence could they find in your week in order to bring charges that would hold up in court?

Over and above attendance at Mass, how are your concrete choices different from a non-believer? Would, say, your choice of career be based on any different motives from his or hers? Would the choice be prompted by an urge to serve or more heavily by income, influence, prestige, material comforts? If you had a business decision, say, to close a plant which was the central source of income for a town, would you be swayed by the effects on the lives of the workers and those who provided them auxiliary services, or would the bottom-line factor be the profit-loss column? If a family had a loan with your bank which they simply couldn't pay now without tragic effects on their lives, would you give them an extension—without penalties? Is it your common practice when you've had a hurtful argument to make peace "before the sun goes down"?

Hard questions, but "I did not come to bring peace, but a sword" (Matthew 10:34).

• (Page 152) This chapter also spoke of three quite broad manifestations of evil in the world today to which we have, maybe without realizing it, hardened ourselves—most likely out of sheer self-defense from the enormity of it: the monstrous evils which overwhelm whole peoples, the utter inhumanities to which the day-to-day reportage has toughened our sensitivities, and the petty everyday indignities which we have come to regard as simply irritating "givens."

Make three columns on a sheet of paper and label them "Monstrous," "Inhuman," "Mean-Spirited." Spend some time— perhaps more than you had originally planned—and fill in the columns.

Is there more evil in the world than you suspected?

Chapter 8

• (Page 161) Readers of these pages, younger or older, will most likely have experienced confirmation already. For most Catholics, even those who no longer practice, it was a memorable occasion, perhaps more for the dress-up and the fuss and the presents, the chance to see a bishop close up, being among the people at the focus of a Church event.

How much of an *internal* impact did it make at the time? Try to remember. Were you old enough that it made you feel more "grown-up," more responsible, a different kind of member in "the Church"?

The eucharist is the sacrament we receive over and over again, to keep the Spirit in us alive. But baptism and confirmation we receive once-for-all. Do those two dramatic events still influence the life of your soul? Do they keep your faith "living, conscious, and active"?

• (Page 175) Imagine that friends of yours have just had a new baby and have asked you to be the child's godparent. After reading the chapter, what goes through your mind before you respond to that invitation?

Chapter 9

• (Page 183) When you have a bad tooth, it's often "tolerable"; it causes distress only every once in awhile; leave it alone and maybe it will take care of itself. What's the only sensible thing to do?

When you watch television and keep channel surfing from one dull program to another and another, do you settle for the least dull, sure that the next program is "bound" to be better, or do you get up and do something completely different?

When you suffer the "blahs," the feeling that life has become little better than one-damn-thing-after-another, what do you do? Do you take charge of your mood and start taking control of your life, or do you merely wait for "something" to show up?

Very honestly, what is your *fundamental option?* For ever-fuller life, or for death-in-life?

• (Page 191) A National Opinion Research Center study in 1964 showed that 38 percent of American Catholics confessed monthly; in 1974, that had declined to 17 percent. And yet in that same period, weekly communion increased from 20 percent to more than 80 percent. What factors would you suspect contributed to that? Are there any hints in the first chapter?

What is your own personal attitude toward sin: your own comfort/discomfort with it? When you've done something undeniably belittling, how to you react? What is your response to the invitation to sit down with a fellow sinner and "have a conversation about sin"? Is your attitude toward God the same as Adam and Eve's: We can get along without you very well?

• (Page 198) Think of a time when, contrary to all your expectations, someone forgave you, a time when you felt graced:

SACRAMENTS: RITES OF PASSAGE 275

loved undeservedly. What had you done, and how did the person you hurt respond?

Think of a time when, with a great deal of fear and embarrassment, you spilled out something shaming in confession, and the priest welcomed you back and made you feel completely free of the guilt. How did it feel? Was the relief when it was over worth the cost of bringing it out into the open?

Think of someone you've had a longtime grudge against. Would it be worth the undeniable discomfort and embarrassment to set both of you free of that burden?

Chapter 10

• (Page 210) Gold and silver are precious because they are rare. Earth, air, water seem to be unimportant—until they are threatened by drought or pollution. Then at least those who are not totally self-absorbed begin to understand their true value.

Without the unwelcome intrusion of suffering—and death, we would take everything for granted. Nothing would be precious. Of course we treasure our families, friends, our own bodies, freedom, work, recreation. Sort of. But they become *intensely* cherished only when we suddenly realize they are threatened.

List—in no particular order—the things you would miss most painfully if they or you were threatened. Then painstakingly put them in order of priority.

• (Page 216) There is no denying that all the Christian rituals that surround death are sad and painful. But imagine that someone you truly loved had died. Try to describe how you would feel *without* him or her: the wake, the vigil, the funeral liturgy, the group of family and friends gathered to support one another at the graveside.

If it helps to prod your imagination, read the opening of Albert Camus' *The Stranger,* in which a young man who believes in no transcendent dimension to human life describes the death of his mother.

Chapter 11

• (Page 232) Mull over what has been said about the priesthood in this chapter, especially what is said about the priesthood of the laity.

Women feel, rightly, underused by the Church they profoundly care for. Although they can now perform some minor functions in the liturgy like reading and distributing communion, they can neither act as celebrants nor contribute meaningfully to Church policy. Then again, most males in the Church find themselves in exactly the same position.

It is not likely that in our lifetime we will see the ordination of women or married men. But you still can be "priestly" in a very real sense. How?

Chapter 12

• (Page 241) Consider the situation addressed in this chapter: the young man asking for a Catholic priest to witness his wedding when he did not practice his faith and intended to bring up his children Jewish. If you were the priest or deacon he approached, would you accept? Why?

Anyone baptized Catholic is a Catholic Christian; that "seal" doesn't go away. But is there a "limit" to those the Church should marry and baptize? Where does one "draw the line"—if at all? To pose the question in another way: If being Catholic were a crime against the state (as it has been in many times and places), what hard, concrete evidence would the state have to find in order to arrest you as a genuine Catholic?

• (Page 250) Not too many people reading these pages are about to get married. But all of us are—or ought to be—in love. Read what St. Paul says about loving and test out your most ardent love against what he says:

> "Love is patient and kind; it is not jealous or conceited or proud; love is not ill-mannered or selfish or irritable; love does not keep a record of wrongs; love is not happy with evil, but is happy with the truth. Love never gives up; and its faith, hope, and patience never fail.
>
> *(1 Corinthians 13:4–7)*

Acknowledgments

Scripture quotations are taken from or adapted from the Good News Bible text, Today's English Version. Copyright © American Bible Society 1966, 1971, 1976, 1992.

The poem by Gerard Manley, S.J. on page 73 is from *Poems of Gerard Manley Hopkins*, 3d ed., edited by W.H. Gardner (New York and London: Oxford University Press, 1948).

Excerpt on page 10 from *J.B.* by Archibald MacLeish, Copyright © 1956, 1957, 1958 by Archibald MacLeish. London, Toronto, Samuel French, Inc.

Excerpt on page 16 from *The Hollow Men* by T. S. Eliot, *Collected Poems 1909-1935*, Copyright 1936 © by Harcourt, Brace & Co, Inc.

Excerpt on page 17 from *The Metamorphosis*, by Franz Kafka, Copyright © by Schocken Books, Inc.

Excerpt on pages 22-25 from *Waiting for Godot* by Samuel Beckett, Copyright © 1954 by Grove Press.

Excerpt on pages 36 and 63-67 from *The Power of Myth* by Joseph Campbell with Bill Moyers, Copyright © 1988 by Apostrophe S Productions, Inc., and Alfred van der Marck Editions, published by Doubleday, New York, NY.

Excerpt on pages 52 and 97 from *The Varieties Of Religious Experience* by William James, Copyright © 1902 by William James, New York: Longmans, Green and Co.

Excerpt on page 59 from *Collected Poems of W. B. Yeats*, Copyright © 1950 by the Macmillan Co.

"The Twelve Steps" are reprinted with permission of Alcoholics Anonymous World Services, Inc. Permission to reprint this material does not mean that AA has reviewed or approved the contents of this publication, nor that AA agrees with the views expressed herein.

Excerpt on pages 91-92 is from *Sleep with Angels* by Mary Fisher, Copyright © by 1994 by Moyer Bell, Wakefield, RI.

Excerpts on various pages are from *The Documents of Vatican II*, Walter M. Abbott, S.J., Gen. Ed. Copyright © 1966 by The America Press.

Excerpt on page 1 from *Is That All there Is?* by Peggy Lee, Copyright 1966 by Yellow Dog Music Inc.,/Hudson Bay Music, Inc., New York, NY.

Excerpt on page 3 is from *Hard Times* by Charles Dickens, Afterword Copyright © 1961 by the New American Library of World Literature, Inc.

Excerpt on page 119 is from *The Man on a Donkey: A Chronicle* by Hilda Frances Margaret Prescott, Copyright © 1952 by H.F.M. Prescott (The MacMillan Company).

Excerpts on pages 157, 194, 195, 211 are from *The Meaning of the Sacraments* by Monika Hellwig, Copyright © 1981 by Pfaum/Standard.

Excerpts on pages 134, 170-172, 204, 238 are from *The New Dictionary of Sacramental Worship*, Peter E. Fink, S.J., Ed.. Copyright © 1990 by The Order of Saint Benedict, Inc., Collegeville, Minnesota (A Michael Glazier Book, The Liturgical Press, Collegeville, Minnesota).

Excerpt on page 223 is from *As One Who Serves*, Copyright © 1977 by UNITED STATES CATHOLIC CONFERENCE.

Excerpts on pages 182 and 183 are from *Sacraments for Secular Man* by George McCauley, S.J., Copyright © 1969 by Herder and Herder, Inc., New York, New York.

Excerpt on page 198 is from *The Christian Commitment* by Karl Rahner, S.J., Copyright © 1963 by Sheed and Ward, Ltd.

Excerpt on page 234 is from *The Skin of Our Teeth* by Thornton Wilder, Copyright © 1952 by Thornton Wilder.

The poem by John Donne on page 264 is from *The Complete Poetry and Selected Prose of John Donne*, edited by M. H. Abrams (New York and London: W. W. Norton and Co., 1979).

Bibliography

In such a text, footnotes are at best intrusive, as are frequent statements such as, "As Peter Berger writes . . . ." Let this list, then, serve as an indication of my grateful indebtedness to the following authors.

Anderson and Fite. *Becoming Married.* John Knox, 1993.

Bellah, Robert, et al. *Habits of the Heart.* Harper and Row, 1985.

Berger, Peter. *A Rumor of Angels.* Anchor, 1970.

Browne, Fishwick, Browne. *Dominant Symbols in Popular Culture.* Bowling Green, 1990.

Campbell, Joseph. *The Power of Myth.* Doubleday, 1988.

Dillistone, F.W. *Christianity and Symbolism.* Westminster, 1955.
———. *The Power of Symbols in Religion and Culture.* Crossroad, 1986.

Douglas, Mary. *Natural Symbols.* Barrie and Rochliff, 1970.

Eliade, Mircea. *The Sacred and the Profane.* Harcourt Brace, 1959.

Fink, S.J., Peter (ed.). *The New Dictionary of Sacramental Worship.* Liturgical Press, 1990.

Guzie, Tad W. *The Book of Sacramental Basics.* Paulist, 1981.

Hitchcock, James. *The Recovery of the Sacred.* Crossroad, 1974.

James, William. *The Varieties of Religious Experience.* Longmans Green, 1902.

Jung, C.G. *Man and His Symbols.* Doubleday, 1964.
———. *Modern Man in Search of a Soul.* Harvest, 1933.
———. *Psychology and Religion.* Yale, 1933.

Langer, Suzanne. *Philosophy in a New Key.* Harvard, 1951.

Lasch, Christopher. *The Culture of Narcissism.* Warner, 1979.

May, Rollo (ed.). *Symbolism in Religion and Literature.* Braziller, 1960.

Moore, Thomas. *Care of the Soul.* Harper, 1992.

Nathanson, Paul. *Over the Rainbow: The Wizard of Oz as a Secular Myth of America.* SUNY Press, 1991.

Otto, Rudolf. *The Idea of the Holy.* Oxford, 1923.

Roszak, Theodore. *Unfinished Animal.* Harper and Row, 1975.

Schillebeeckx, Edward. *Christ: The Sacrament of the Encounter with God.* Sheed and Ward, 1963.

Verhalen, Philip. *Faith in a Secularized World.* Paulist, 1976.